MW00966051

One Big Fib

One Big Fib

◆

The Incredible Story of the Fraudulent First International Bank of Grenada

OWEN PLATT

iUniverse, Inc.
New York Lincoln Shanghai

One Big Fib
The Incredible Story of the Fraudulent First International Bank of Grenada

iUniverse, Inc.

For information address:
iUniverse, Inc.
2021 Pine Lake Road, Suite 100
Lincoln, NE 68512
www.iuniverse.com

ISBN: 0-595-28298-9 (pbk)
ISBN: 0-595-65755-9 (cloth)

Printed in the United States of America

Contents

"And what will be the paid up capital of The Anglo-Bengalee Disinterested Loan and Life Insurance Company?"
"A figure of two and as many noughts after it as the printer can get into the same line!"

—from Martin Chuzzlewit by Charles Dickens, 1844.

Introduction

Gilbert Allen Ziegler, later to be known as Van Arthur Brink, perpetrated what must be the most cynical banking fraud in history. The banks that he founded, without any tangible capital, robbed innumerable people of their savings, and in many cases, of their future. Contacted for his comments at the start of research for this book, he asked that "the book be objective" in its approach to the subject as a condition of his cooperation. As research proceeded, it became apparent that his definition of objectivity would probably not coincide with the conclusions being reached, and thus his comments are restricted to some of the innumerable outpourings he publishes over the Internet to this day.

Much of the content is drawn from public records and from postings on the Internet bulletin boards, many of the numerous documents produced by the First Bank and its acolytes themselves being reproduced in full, as this seemed the only way to illustrate adequately the duplicity of their actions. I am deeply indebted to those former clients of First Bank and its subsidiaries who have been good enough to supply information from their personal experience. This has not been easy for them as their relationship with the bank has left its mark, not only financially, but also mentally upon many.

Sadly, this book can in no way compensate them for their losses but it may, perhaps, encourage the forces of law enforcement to continue their efforts to apprehend the guilty.

Credit must be given to the British writer, David Marchant, whose monthly publication, Offshore Alert, was ultimately responsible in forcing the Government of Grenada to take action, albeit reluctantly and far too late. Brash, belligerent but invariably correct, he has waged a lengthy battle against fraud in the offshore financial world. It is a pity that so many of those defrauded by First Bank and Van Brink, did not have access to his writings or, if they did, ignored his warnings. Thanks are also due to the many journalists whose contributions did much to assist in putting together the jigsaw puzzle that was The First Bank of Grenada.

In the case of depositors with First Bank, greed seems to have outweighed commonsense and reason. The promoters played upon this, their investment ignorance and their religious gullibility to create the biggest swindle of all time in offshore banking.

The sheer complexity of the organisation means that many details, mainly of the affairs of some of the lesser sub-banks whose operations mirrored those of the others, have had to be omitted and undoubtedly some matters have been over-looked, for which I apologise. The understandable reticence of some former clients to come forward with information has been a handicap, as has been the problem of sorting fact from fiction in many of the statements made concerning the convoluted affairs of the banks concerned.

Undoubtedly the book will not please Van Brink. But it can claim to be thoroughly objective as he had requested. For all his verbose protestations and blustering he has yet to produce a shred of hard evidence to convince anyone that his bank was anything other than a grandiose confidence trick. Nowhere is there the slightest indication that the The First International Bank of Grenada ever carried on anything that could be remotely described as legitimate "banking business."

From start to finish, it was all One Big Fib.

"If you want to steal money, buy a bank."

—Berthold Brecht.

"Only two things are infinite—the universe and human stupidity, and I'm not so sure about the universe."

—Albert Einstein

1

A Wedding in Kampala

If you were thinking of having a wedding in Uganda, January would be a pretty good month to choose for it. The temperatures are pleasant, the humidity is low, it being a dry season, and gentle breezes blow in the higher elevations such as in the capital city of Kampala, perched 3700 feet up on a range of hills a mere 40 kms. away from the lush shores of Lake Victoria.

January 20th, 2001 was no meteorological exception to this general rule and the fine weather must have seemed a good omen to the guests assembled in the luxury of the downtown Kampala Sheraton Hotel. Plain clothes security men, some from the Sheraton's own staff and others recruited elsewhere, patrolled the corridors to ensure that no unwanted intruders invaded the privacy of this gala event and the flags atop the hotel fluttered decorously in the pleasant afternoon breeze.

Among the predominantly white guest list, invited by way of E-Mail, were some local celebrities such as Maj. Gen Salim Saleh, Bonny Katatumba, Chairman of Uganda's Chamber of Commerce, Dr. Ian Clarke, Wasswa and Yogi Birigwa, mayoral candidate for Kampala and his wife, all awaiting the arrival of the couple whose wedding earlier that week was the occasion for this lavish champagne reception.

At two o'clock, an eggshell white four wheel drive Jeep Cherokee with Congolese licence plates number KV46670D spun into the driveway and a buzz of expectation ran through the assembly outside the Rwenzori ball room. From the car emerged a slightly over-weight and balding white male bridegroom in his fifties, a young, very young, Ugandan bride plus two even younger Ugandan bridesmaids and a patriachally white bearded individual who was performing the traditional function of being best man for the occasion.

Acknowledging the plaudits of the crowd, the couple were swept into the ballroom for a gala celebration of the ceremony that the bridegroom, Van Arthur Brink formerly Gilbert Allen Ziegler, fugitive ex-banker, conman and bankrupt, fervently hoped would secure his future residence in Uganda by reason of his marriage to Annet Asiimwe, one time barfly at the Sheraton's Rhino Bar. In her picture, the bride certainly looked less than enthusiastic about her new role as the spouse of the man at the head of the biggest banking swindle of the century if not of all time, but must have reasoned that it was probably going to be better than hanging out in the hotel bar.

Further lustre was added to the occasion by having appointed one, Douglas Ferguson, as best man for the occasion. Ferguson, a Canadian, had run a totally fraudulent insurance operation in the Caribbean island of Nevis and later in Dominica in conjunction with Brink to insure, allegedly, the deposits of clients of his bank.

A mere eight days before, Brink's bank, the imperiously named First International Bank of Grenada, had been put into liquidation with debts of some $472 million, mostly owing to defrauded clients.

And what an occasion this was!

Kampala had rarely seen such an opulent extravagance since the days of the unlamented Idi Amin. A minor scuffle when security guards stopped a reporter and photographer from the New Vision paper from attending did little to mar the occasion. The photographer's camera was seized and his film confiscated for fear that it might contain a picture of the fugitive banker, after which the party resumed.

After all, for an occasion such as this, no expense should be spared.

After all, it wasn't their money they were spending!

Several thousand miles away, people, mostly Americans and Canadians, were putting their lives back together having seen their investments, often their life savings, disappear into the maw of the First International Bank of Grenada and thus into Van Brink's pocket. Lured by promises of returns of up to 250% on their investment, they had poured money into the coffers of Van Brink and his henchmen. Assured that their funds were fully secured by the totally sham corporation, The International Deposit Insurance Corporation, also the brainchild of Brink, few questioned just how these returns could possibly be generated, and the money rolled in.

While there was a steady influx of fresh investors standing in line to put up their money, things rolled along merrily. A few lucky ones even managed to extract some of their cash from the bank in the early days but with the inflow drying up, as Mr. Ponzi had found many years before, things get a bit sticky in the fraud department.

With exquisite timing, Mr. Van Brink ostensibly resigned from his position as major domo at the bank, packed his bags and removed himself from Grenada to Uganda. By the time the full magnitude of the disaster had entered the consciousness of the somnolent and compliant regulators in Grenada, it was all over.

The liquidator, Marcus Wide of Price Waterhouse and Co. was left to struggle with the impossible task of making some sense out of the shambles that was left. By this time the other principals in the operation had wisely decamped and he was left to do what he could with some very inadequate records—and no funds.

"It is always the best policy to speak the truth—unless, of course, you are an exceptionally good liar."

—Jerome K. Jerome (1859–1927)

2

The Leopard's Spots

"Hillsboro has old-fashioned charm, yet is only 20 minutes away from the big city amenities of Portland. It offers a variety of parks, fairs, historical places and rural beauty that can appeal to any visitor's taste. Hillsboro is the government seat of Washington County, a fast growing area of Oregon. But, people there still share a smile and extend a friendly welcome to newcomers."

Thus runs the introduction on the website of this small Oregon town. Among its former citizens, one, Gilbert Ziegler's name would probably no longer raise a smile amongst the good burghers of that town having become their most famous, or infamous, son. But there was little in the early life of the young Ziegler to indicate that he would one day be at the centre of one of the world's biggest banking swindles. On the face of it, his curriculum vitae, although distinctly lacking in verifiable detail, showed little out of the ordinary for the first forty years of his life even with the imaginative details that appear to have been added to spice it up:

"Was born in Seattle, Washington, USA, on February 4, 1951. I am the third of four children. My father was a Seventh Day Adventist minister. My mother was the author of Christian children's books.
Both of my parents are now deceased.

He continues to expound upon his life long love of music, adding that "I still enjoy a Karaoke party on occasions", an unusual addiction for a music lover. Later his fertile imagination becomes more apparent for, according to his resumé, he had earned at least six degrees, including a doctorate in divinity and a Ph.D. in economics, all from Green River Community College in Auburn, Washington. However this college does not offer any full degree programmes or post-graduate degrees and has no divinity department, making his academic achievement there all the more remarkable. He becomes equally creative when he moves on to his professional career, where, in spite of his lack of recognisable degrees, he claims to have taught philosphy and economics at an un-named college in Oregon.

> *1974-1977 Assistant to the President for a private business college.*
> *Was responsible for media promotions, college publications, government relations, accreditation, curriculum development, library development and for lobbying the state legislature and regulatory bodies so that private business schools would have the right to grant Associate of Science degrees. My college became the first business college in Oregon to gain degree-granting authority. Also taught Economics, History of Economic Philosophy, Advertising, Report Writing, and Journalism. Student population grew from an average of 85-125 to 375-450.*

Unfortunately, the name of this outstanding establishment has been omitted and remains something of a mystery but his next venture, albeit a brief one, was a memorable career change:

> *1977 Partner, fast food restaurant (Mexican menu).*

From Tacos it was a rather less than obvious leap back to a previous career, a return to academics:

> *1978 At age 27, I became the youngest president of a degree-granting college in the nation. The college subsequently won national accreditation honors for having the finest library in the nation for a college of its type and size. The passive investor-owner sold the school to another group that instituted programmed learning (cassette teaching tapes) in place of teachers. I left shortly thereafter. Enrollments dropped, forcing the new owners to close the school a few years later.*

Sadly, the name of yet another outstanding educational gem has been omitted and a search for this failed to locate the college or the fate of this great library.

> *1978-81 Founder/Creative Director for a regional advertising agency. Took on a couple partners. Company grew to a full-time staff of nine when I sold.*
> *1981-83 Concert promotions and business consulting.*
> *1984-86 Church administrator, choir director, bible teacher of a small fellowship of about 100. Organized a food bank which grew to serving 1,200 families weekly and was featured on the 700 Club television show. Church attendance grew to 750.*
> *1986-89 Church pastor, founder and president of a non-denominational organization of Christian fellowships that has now grown to over 50 participating fellowships internationally (last I heard, two years ago).*

1989-92 Executive Vice President—Loan Underwriting Department of a mortgage banking company. Company received state recognition as one of Oregon's Top-10 Growth Companies in 1991. In 1992 the staff size grew to nearly 100 with a service area covering two states.

1992-94 Rather than see the company fold and everyone let go from employment, I took over ownership by signing personal guarantees on all corporate debt. I was unsuccessful in my efforts at revitalizing the company, due to lack of capitalization, and was forced into personal bankruptcy in January 1994. The bankruptcy was discharged in May 1994. Over the course of five years the company had originated some $400 million in mortgage loans."

This would hardly seem to have been much of a recommendation for the fiscal acumen of the future owner of a bank that would, in a few years time, claim to have an asset base of $54 billion! And the bankruptcy had not been discharged as he claimed.

Unfortunately, as with many of his later statements, there is a distinct absence of verifiable detail in his history and at least one major omission, but the folksy, self-deprecating charm he exhibits here will stand him in good stead in later years when he talks hundreds of investors into putting their trust and dollars into his First International Bank of Grenada and their ancillary institutions.

By 1994, however, a bankrupt Ziegler was en route to Hawaii to start a new life, almost certainly motivated by an incident conveniently missing from his *curriculum vitae*, an Oregon state investigation into securities fraud related to an offshore trust. Although charges were never pressed, clearly it was time to move along. According to the *Los Angeles Times*, an affidavit filed in that case by a state investigator charged that Ziegler recruited investors to subscribe to an offshore newsletter for $150. Each subscriber was encouraged to recruit new subscribers. Part of the money from new subscriptions would be added to the original subscriber's offshore account. The original subscriber could never get his hands on the money, according to the affidavit, but it was supposed to grow and be passed along to the subscriber's heirs some day. A sense of the sales pitch can be gleaned from an affidavit from an Oregon securities investigator, Vasilios Karalekas. Acting on a tip from a local preacher, he attended a meeting in Lake Oswego, Ore., promoting something called the Private Legacy Trust. According to the affidavit, filed in 1998 in state court in Washington County, Ore., at the meeting, Mr. Brink (while still known as Gil Ziegler) "told us how we could all be making millions of dollars every year once we joined by subscribing to an offshore newsletter and contributing $150 to an irrevocable account in an offshore bank."

As explained, each client would get additional money added to his or her account by attracting three more clients, who would then attract three more clients, and so on; the depositor couldn't withdraw the principal, but it would grow in this manner into a tidy sum for the depositor's heirs someday. Mr. Karalekas said in the affidavit that he believed the group was committing "securities fraud." The case was turned over to the U.S. attorney's office for further investigation.

As Ziegler's bankruptcy statement showed assets of $28,440 and liabilities of $1,144,084 with an income of $850 and expenditure of $845, it might make one wonder how he paid for his ticket to Hawaii! The Oregon investigators probably had the same thought in mind when they found that he had vanished. In fact, he had partly financed the move by borrowing $25,000 from Mary Merker, a retired Oregon schoolteacher who later said, "he was very charismatic." He promised she would be repaid once he didn't have to sleep on the beach any more and had money to feed himself. "He gave me this song and dance," she says. "He claimed he was in abject poverty." In spite of many promises, the debt was never repaid.

In Hawaii, where by his own account he claims to have been an "offshore consultant", presumably on the basis of his earlier sales of offshore newsletters and the peddling of a worthless trust, he made a startling economic recovery, one suspects courtesy of the Private Legacy Trust and Mrs. Merker. By 1996, using as a nominee a long-haired young lady, Cynthia Hastey, who rejoiced in the nickname "Tai", he was able to buy a bank licensed in Nauru for a trifling $50,000, a triumph for someone so bankrupt a year or two previously. For those who are not familiar with the island nation of Nauru (and not many are), until recently it had depended for its livelihood upon the ample deposits of Guano fertiliser littering the place. Realising that manure is not forever nor for everyone, the 8000 inhabitants cast about for an additional source of income and hit upon licensing offshore banks as a money-spinner. Better still, by granting bank licences without too much in the way of formal requirements apart from money, they found plenty of takers and soon the 7.7 square mile island was awash with dubious banks, Ziegler's Fidelity International Bank being one of them.

Purchased from a Canadian purveyor of paper banking licences, Gilbert Ziegler, whose previous banking experience appears to have been counting the takings at The Helping Hand Ministry and presiding over the failure of Hometown Mortgage, was now an international banker—except that, in order to preserve an "arm's length" status from himself, Ms. Hastey, a former cosmetics store clerk at Mana Foods in Maui, who seems to have been having a difficult love life at the time, became transmogrified into the owner of the bank, something of a startling transformation. Bruce and Sandra Jeddeloh with whom he was staying at the time had introduced her to Ziegler. The Jeddelohs (he was something of a computer whiz and helped out with setting up the Internet presence for the bank) had then become a part of the empire designed to market the bank and its products to a gullible public. A Danny Hashimoto also played a leading role in the cosy coterie. It seems that much of the inspiration for the building of the structure that was to eventually emerge as The First International Bank of Grenada came from this tight knit group surrounding Ziegler, many of whom seem to have been involved in rather dubious business activities prior to his arrival. Ziegler appears to have been the catalyst, a part that he played well, and Fidelity Bank the vehicle to enable them to move on to bigger and better things. As yet they were marking time to some extent with the newly acquired Fidelity Bank which had only a Class B Banking Licence, a restriction that meant that all transactions had to go through a correspondent bank with a Class A Licence, and for the now upwardly mobile and rising Gilbert Ziegler, this was a severe handicap to his aspirations. Casting about for a suitable jurisdiction that would provide him with an unrestricted banking licence with few questions asked, his gaze was drawn toward Grenada.

Grenada, at the bottom end of The Caribbean was mostly famous for its spices and for the dubiously legal conquest by the United States to prevent a Communist regime taking hold. Economically, as with many small and now independent jurisdictions, times were hard. Once again, as Nauru had perceived, providing facilities for offshore banks and international business companies seemed like a gift from heaven. Once again, sweeping aside restrictive controls was the secret to attracting so many prospective offshore banking barons in the style of Gilbert Ziegler.

In spite of the restriction of a Class B Licence, Fidelity was doing well, encouraging depositors with well above average returns on the nebulous investment products offered, but the continual oversight of another bank who might at any moment enquire into the validity of some of the high yielding investments on sale, seriously cramped its style. Promoted through so-called "wealth seminars" in Boulder, Colorado with titles such as Infinite Asset Management, some trusty cohorts, including Ms. Hastey and the Jeddelohs, pitched their sales talk to naïve investors who were attracted by the lack of governmental oversight, invaluable if you were a tax evader, and the sparkling (and unrealisable) financial returns offered, attractive if you wished to become almost instantly wealthy. "A New Paradigm in Banking" was the catch phrase. Added glitz was displayed in the form of a due diligence letter on an attorney's letterheading, testifying to the good standing and sound financial asset base of Fidelity International Bank. The attorney just happened to be a personal friend.

The United States had successfully separated church and state in their constitution but had been far less successful in separating church and con man and Gil Ziegler's quasi-religious background was brought into full play to sell the bank as a service for the good of mankind. Bankers are not usually regarded as benevolent and charitable beings but Fidelity, insisted Ziegler, was different. Not only would the clients benefit from the huge interest rates on deposits but so would mankind in general. It was a persuasive pitch to many and Ziegler brought all the skills to it that had made The Helping Hands Ministry a success, based on the principal that The Lord helps them who help themselves.

However, without a physical presence the bank was virtually in cyberspace, courtesy of the Internet, all the "back office" work being performed by a master bank uncontrolled by Ziegler, a serious handicap if you are going to play fast and loose with depositor's money. Not at all the image he needed nor an arrangement that would give him the degree of flexibility he desired.

The Dominion of Melchizedek offered one of the banking possibilities that he had investigated previously. This totally spurious "Dominion" had been founded by an absconding felon, allegedly deceased although there seems to be some doubt as to this, and now proclaimed itself as an ecclesiastical nation complete with its own bible and a gamut of imaginitive ministeries and officers. Although somewhat handicapped by having no bit of territory it could call its own, it issued passports, citizenships and, naturally, banking licences, all promoted through an elaborate website! These last were eagerly snapped up by those seeking an easy entry into the world of high finance only to find that, in spite of the lofty claims of the Dominion, the rest of the world's bankers remained obtusely unaware of their validity. In order to do banking business, it is necessary to come to some arrangement with a major international financial institution in order to get your funds into the monetary system. Faced with the refusal to touch a Melchizedekian bank with the equivalent of a banking bargepole, the proud owners of these were left holding some expensive bits of useless paper. Ziegler knew enough of the business to realise that this was not the answer but he did go along with their passport programme and Gilbert Allen Ziegler, late of Oregon, U.S.A., was soon the proud holder of a Melchizedek passport, an impressive looking document bearing the mighty seal of that non-existent state. So impressed were Melchizedek with him or he with them that he was appointed in no time to be Ambassador at Large (Caribbean) and his name was proudly displayed on their website immediately beneath that of another "banker", one Peter Drakoulakolos, who had also previously made a hurried exit from the United States for dubious financial reasons (he was running a phony Melchizedekian bank) and was now Ambassador at Large (South America).

With a Melchizedekian passport in his back pocket, Ziegler homed in on an unsuspecting and innocent Grenada. The leopard was not changing his spots, just re-locating.

"Don't steal. The government hates competition."

—Anon.

3

Very Private Banking

Say "offshore bank" to the average person and they immediately conjure up an image of a sleazy underworld of financial chicanery and wrongdoing. This perception is unfortunate, to say the least, to the image of a great many offshore banks that are highly reputable and law abiding. Offshore is a mis-nomer in any case. It is used to describe the use by a citizen of one country of the banking resources of another, frequently on the grounds of privacy but often to shield some nefarious activity from the citizen's own authorities or even from his wife. But offshore it does not have to be. Switzerland, for many years a bastion of very private and anonymous banking can hardly be described as offshore from anywhere, but the fortunes of Swiss banks were built upon that very foundation of privacy.

The dismantling of empires, principally Great Britain's, threw many lesser countries back onto their own, usually negligible resources. No longer propped up by the economics and managerial experience of the mother country and generally pretty lacking in international knowhow, with a few notable exceptions their financial health declined. Years previously, The Bahamas had been described to The Duke of Windsor, then Governor of those islands, as "a pimple on the arse of the British Empire" and this could probably have been applied to most of the possessions that were happily relinquished, if officially reluctantly, in the cause of independence after World War II.

Becoming independent is a bit like leaving home without a job to go to and the newly formed nations cast about for means to supplement their incomes, white sandy beaches and bananas being insufficient to sustain life in the face of the onslaught of consumerism from abroad by way of television and other intrusive media.

The British Virgin Isles, technically still part of the British Empire (it became a British Dependency, not a self-governing independent nation), can be credited with the introduction of a moneyspinner for such nations. They invented the

International Business Company, (I.B.C.), a structure which enabled companies to be incorporated cheaply, quickly and, most importantly, anonymously. There were no awkward questions as to ownership, no financial statements to be filed annually or at all, and no reporting of any kind to anyone—complete and utter privacy. If any questions were asked, the information was limited to the date of incorporation and the name and address of the required Registered Agent for the company, usually a local lawyer. Local law forbade any other disclosure. Even better, these jurisdictions would not recognise foreign judgements making them secure boltholes for anyone at risk from litigation, a great attraction for citizens of that most litigious of nations, the United States. Doctors, dentist, chiropractors and even lawyers found placing their assets in an offshore company was considerably more cost efficient than paying for malpractice insurance—and just as effective. It produced an instant bonanza for BVI and other nations took note. Before long a whole range of independent island nations had plagiarised their IBC act and become purveyors in their own right. For those seeking anonymity in business for whatever reason, it was a Godsend and money flowed into the coffers of both the governments and the Registered Agents. The Bahamas, Cayman, St.Kitts and Nevis, St. Vincent & The Grenadines, Montserrat, St Lucia, Anguilla and Grenada were among those who incorporated the IBC Act in their constitutions as a fillip to their national revenues.

Hand in hand with the new legislation went the need for banks to service the hundreds of IBC's being formed. A handful of recognisable international banks were already present such as Barclays, CIBC, Bank of Nova Scotia and CitiBank and these conformed to the rules of privacy that applied to IBC's. No details of accounts or of the beneficial owners of accounts could be divulged without the applicant for the information going through the court system, an almost impossible procedure in any of these jurisdictions, so privacy was strictly preserved. However, the major banks had a few rules of their own. Rules that, to some extent, hampered the laissez faire attitude and privacy that the owners of many IBCs wished to utilise. Banks would ask for verification of the true identity of the client, references from previous banks, genuine addresses of the beneficial owners of the companies, use to which the account would be put and generally attempted to ensure that the account would be used for legitimate and non-criminal activity. Whilst not always successful at combating the improper use of offshore accounts, they were sufficiently rigorous to provide a stumbling block to the true seeker of personal privacy, especially when it related to the tax inspector or some nefarious activity.

Enter the Offshore Banking Licence legislation. Who can claim credit for this innovative bit of thinking is not clear but the idea took off in a big way. By making it possible for Mr. Average to become a banker by merely buying a licence to do banking for himself and for others, it seemed to be an admirable adjunct to the thriving IBC business. Naturally the price was substantial but then so would be the advantages to the purchaser. He could avoid all the stuffy bureaucratic paperwork that the big boys demanded and accept money from whomsoever he pleased with practically no questions asked. No financial experience of any kind was required. All you needed was to provide some very basic details and pay your money—you were an international banker almost overnight or as long as it took your cheque to clear and the FedEx package to reach you.

The little volcanic island of Monserrat in The Caribbean seized upon this idea in a big way (they had little else to seize upon) and the issuance of paper bank licences reached epic proportions. So great was the boom in new offshore banks that the island was dubbed "Monster Rat" by the legitimate banking community. Soon the fraudulent and improper use of these "banks" became such that the government were forced to rescind nearly every licence that had been issued and Monserrat retreated in some ignominy from the international financial scene. The volcano that decimated the island a few years later was regarded by much of the professional banking world as merely divine intervention.

Nauru, an insignificant dot in the Pacific was another location for easy bank acquisition but was seriously hampered by being almost unreachable by prospective clients, although this was not always the disadvantage it might seem to banks whose substance might be questionable. The jurisdiction did offer the immense advantage to the new banker that the "capital" requirement of $100,000 did not have to appear in the books for two years and then only on paper—it did not have to be on deposit in Nauru—rendering it totally worthless as a safeguard for depositors. Internet, relatively new on the scene, filled the communication gap admirably for such banks. A flashy website cost practically nothing to set-up and thousands were gulled into thinking cyberspace banks had a real presence. Bricks and mortar were replaced with clicks and E-Mail.

Other offshore nations were keen to get on the bandwagon—and Grenada, now firmly fixed in Gilbert Ziegler's sights, was one of them.

"The entire essence of America is the hope to first make money—then make money with money—then make lots of money with lots of money."

—Paul Erdman

4

The Spice Islands

Grenada's claim to fame lay largely in its principal product, spices, an export commodity that was unlikely to fill the fiscal bill when the nation became independent. Tourism, hardly developed, was not aided when the United States elected to invade the islands ostensibly to displace a communist government in 1983 but more realistically to divert attention from the recent terrorist attack on the US Embassy in Beruit. The assault brought howls of protest from around the globe (and more importantly from British Prime Minister Margaret Thatcher) at this wanton disregard of U.K. sovereignty but did help the US, frustrated by their inability to topple Cuba's Castro, to claim a victory, however miniscule, in their crusade against the Evil Empire. It must have been a relief to the White House to see US Marines conquering anything at all after their recent rebuff in Viet Nam, although the fact that some of the forces were recruited from other Eastern Caribbean states was discreetly played down. The US government had convinced a handful of Caribbean nations to pledge support for a US invasion of the island. US forces invaded six days later in an operation that claimed the lives of 70 Cubans, 42 Americans and 170 Grenadians, including 18 who were killed when US forces mistakenly bombed the island's mental hospital instead of a rebel stronghold. Most US forces withdrew two months later, although a joint US-Caribbean force remained stationed on the island for several years.

15 years later, a democratic government was wrestling with how to provide for its people. The newly instituted IBC Act and the Banking Act were recent innovations in 1996 and, so far, had had few takers. Until Gilbert Allen Ziegler arrived.

Prior to abandoning their imperial island assets, the British had done little to ensure that their successors were well versed in the nuances of governmental and commercial chicanery. Fine colonial governors though they may have been, they had delegated comparatively little authority to local talent leaving behind something of an administrative vacuum when they left. Finding competent staff is hard enough in a nation of millions so with a population of around 100,000, Grenada was struggling to find suitably qualified candidates for their government posts.

The newly founded financial services industry was particularly lacking in know-whow and, it subsequently transpired, commonsense. Scouting about for likely candidates to fill the post of arbiter of the destinies of the new banking system, they found a Grenadian, Michael Creft, who had been working for 25 years as an economic analyst in the Manitoba Department of Highways in Canada. Neither he nor the Prime Minister Keith Mitchell, who was acting as Finance Minister at the time, had any prior banking experience but nonetheless he was offered the task of heading up Grenada's Banking Regulatory system in 1997. Michael Creft's department, The Registrar of Financial Services, had a grand total of two employees, one of whom was Michael Creft himself. It was to prove a disastrous appointment.

About this time, a Canadian by the name of Larry Barnabe, had set up shop in another island, St. Kitts, leasing the Fort Thomas Hotel from the government. Hotel management appears not to have been his forte, however, since he very soon decamped, allegedly taking some of the fixtures and fittings with him along with the insurance money paid to repair the hotel after a recent hurricane. In the meantime he had established a little business setting up IBC's for clients using the recently introduced legislation. Grenada looked to be a suitably tolerant environ-ment for his sort of operation (St. Kitts, even before he removed the furniture, wasn't) and Barnabe soon moved in to become an offshore guru to a naïve Gren-adian government.

Barnabe could certainly claim, quite legitimately, that he had some expertise in the area of finance, having been fined and placed on probation by the Cana-dian Ontario Securities Commission for running fake investment schemes and promoting phony offshore condo developments, an expertise that he probably did not bother to mention to the government of Grenada.

As nobody had any experience or sufficient knowledge of the Offshore Sector, the Government elected to engage Larry Barnabe to draft amendments and new Acts to update the insufficient Offshore Legislation dating from 1989 and 1991. So in 1996 Larry Barnabe drafted the required documents leaning heavily on the existing Acts in other Jurisdictions (the Bahamas, Nevis and St-Kitts, Dominica, etc.), Acts which were immediately gratefully accepted by The Grenadian Gov-ernment of Keith Mitchell, and, after a polishing up and legal knocking into shape, were brought to The Senate and the House of Representatives. They duly approved all of the new acts plus a later one written to amend unclear legislation and to make the International Companies Act more competitive with neighbouring jurisdictions. At the same time another money-spinner that Larry Barnabe helped develop and implement was an Economic Citizenship Programme for Grenada. His assistant, David Springer, ex-boyfriend of his daughter and formerly working as a pool cleaner at the hotel in St. Kitts in spite of his MBA, helped draft the documents and create a marketable package for foreign investors who wished to acquire, for whatever reason, Grenadian citizenship. In exchange for the work Larry Barnabe was granted exclusive rights to market the "Second Citizenship Program" and was able to make a substantial profit doing so.

Encouraged by his success in writing the regulations, in 1997, he launched Grenada International Bank and Trust Corp., Grenada's first offshore bank. It proved to be still born. Although raising over $2 million in deposits, most of which then disappeared, a disgruntled employee complained to the regulators that its capital was fake, comprising only uncut gemstones and land in California. True to later form, the regulators ignored the complaint but a lawsuit was then filed against the bank by a depositor, forcing it into liquidation.

It was of little consequence, for the government then authorised Barnabe's newly formed Granite Registry Services to act as the sole authority on behalf of Grenada for the issuance of IBC's and to perform due diligence upon applicants for bank and trust licences, an incredible decision in view of his past record, conferring upon him carte blanche to print money for both himself and his new patrons. Now all Grenada needed was the business.

"Lack of money is no obstacle. Lack of an idea is an obstacle."

—Ken Hakuta

5

Fresh Fields

As he stepped down from the plane onto the tarmac of Grenada's modern, Cuban built, Point Salinas International Airport, Gilbert Ziegler might well have felt that he was touched by the wings of destiny. Almost from his first encounter with Grenadian authority a warm glow had come over him. Grenadian Immigration Authorities at the time were so pleased to see visitors to their island that citizens from other countries were allowed in without passports, merely needing to prove that they were citizens of somewhere. Gilbert Ziegler was admitted as a citizen of a non-existent Dominion of Melchizedek, complete with gold embossed passport, without even the flicker of an official eyelid, and from that moment he must have realised that here was a country he could manipulate to his advantage.

Self styled international banker Ziegler set about the task of ingratiating himself with the authorities, projecting the success of his Nauru bank as a delectable carrot for a government anxious to develop a banking industry.

In these small island nations, expatriates tend to seek association with other expatriates and he quickly made himself known to the owner of Granite Registry Services, a man very much in his own mould. Larry Barnabe was an obvious choice as a sparring partner in his new enterprise and, aided by the registration facilities provided by Granite Services, an application was made firstly for an IBC, which was incorporated on the 2nd.of October 1997, and then for a full, unrestricted banking licence. A minor problem was that the application had to be accompanied by evidence of at least U.S.$2.26 million in capital resources and now Ziegler's creative juices spilled over. Even with the investor's funds from Fidelity Bank, this figure was out of reach but the regulators of banking in Grenada were so bedazzled by him and his tales of success with Fidelity Bank that, almost unbelievably, they settled for a minimal amount of cash ($110,000) and a load of forged documents. A mere seven days later, the First International Bank of Grenada became a licensed entity, the licence being signed by The Honourable Keith Mitchell, Prime Minister, himself. In keeping with Ziegler's policy of a prudent arm's length association with anything dubious, the documents concerning the new bank's assets were not even held by the bank but letters of assignment (in most cases, photo-copies) were produced as evidence of their existence. The assets of Fidelity Bank were assigned, unaudited, to the new bank and, by fiscal sleight of hand, unassisted by any competent outside agency, the registered capital of The First Bank of Grenada ballooned to an impressive sum in excess of $35 million. Much of this was due to the assignment from Fidelity Bank of a ruby, valued at $20 million but discounted for accountancy purposes for a quick sale to a modest $15 million. This in turn had been assigned to Fidelity from a Nevada company called Resource Enhancement. The Grenadian authorities accepted at face value a photocopy of the valuation and of the assignment as proof of the gem's existence and asked for no other verification.

So in October 1997, Ziegler's Fidelity Bank, which had been a nebulous entity at best, was transformed into a Class A institution, The First International Bank of Grenada with the blessing of the government of Grenada and premises on Young Street in the capital city of St. Georges.

St. Georges is regarded, especially by Grenadians, as the most beautiful city in the Caribbean and they are quite right. It does, however, lack the tall buildings and impressive facades normally associated with major banking institutions, two stories being about the most that local construction has aspired to. As a slogan on the wall of the cheaply furbished and modest office of The First International Bank of Grenada stated, "There are no elevators to the house of success—you must climb the stairs". Which was true, proving to be one of the bank's more reliable statements. But, it was hoped, visitors to climb the narrow stairs to the cramped waiting room would be few and far between. For the sort of banking envisaged by First Bank, depositors were better kept, not only at arm's length, but preferably at several thousand miles length for comfort.

Tai Hastey and the crew from Maui and Nevada arrived to help establish the new enterprise but it was not until March of 1998 that the first trickle of funds appeared in the coffers of the bank.

The delay was due to the necessity of setting up another, and this time, totally fictitious, company to attract clients. Investors are chary of putting their money into obscure banks and, especially in the United States, are comforted by the assurances of the Federal Investment Deposit Corporation (FDIC) which guaranteed that investors with member banks would be assured that up to $100,000 of their cash was safe and secure. Whilst the amount would not have done much for a major investor, it was a considerable comfort to the lesser punter and seemed like an excellent scheme to the board of the new bank.

Sadly, their new enterprise would hardly have stood up to any scrutiny by an organisation such as the FDIC even had they been otherwise eligible but this was no impediment to the inventiveness of management. On the 4th.of January 1978, a contract was signed with the International Deposit Insurance Corporation in Nevis, W.I. guaranteeing the full extent of deposits, plus interest, made with FIBG and awarding the bank a "AAA" rating. IDIC had an innovative approach to insurance. Although accepting substantial premiums from the bank, these were not used to insure the deposits as with conventional insurance. These were to be covered by the bank assigning alleged assets, "blocked and lodged" in the wording of the contract, to IDIC which were to be liquidated and used in the case of any default. As has been seen, the assets of FIBG were, to be kind about it, ethereal and whilst they may have been good enough to fool the government of Grenada, would hardly have done much to impress a regular insurance company.

This was hardly necessary. IDIC had been the brainchild of Ziegler and his old pal and sometime houseguest Douglas Ferguson, who was now the nominal head of the "insurance" company. Nevis had been selected as a good jurisdiction for such an enterprise being eager to attract offshore companies and, with a population hovering around the 10,000 mark, was physically incapable of regulating the many new companies springing up. As with most companies registered there, IDIC never had a physical presence at all and most certainly was not registered as an insurance company, the address being that of an incorporater of offshore companies located in an office complex, the Heritage Plaza on Main Street in the capital of Charlestown. The company had been incorporated as Independent Deposit Re-Insurance Company to avoid having to fulfil the requirements of an insurance licence, the "Re" bit being conveniently and improperly dropped later in correspondence. A document, after the "company" had been thrown out of Nevis and moved temporarily to a lawyer's office in Dominica, gives the name as Independent Deposit Indemnity Corporation with no mention or explanation for the change in title.

The contract, amateurishly worded though it was, certainly might have assuaged the concerns of the future clients of FIBG with a requirement of a 3 to 1 ratio of assets to deposits. The modus operandi is explained in the first paragraph of the contract, presumably for the comfort of investors.

> *"The bank understands that the basis and nature of the IDIC "deposit insurance"*
> *is accomplished through administrative and oversight services provided by IDIC*
> *over certain required assets, as defined herein. These assets are either owned by, or*
> *under the lawful custodial care and management of and by the bank. The bank,*
> *therefore, is basically engaged in a form of "self-insurance" by virtue of pledged*

assets either owned or managed by the bank. IDIC's role is that of administrator and "watchdog" over such assets and the management activities of the bank. This role includes independent verification of the existence, value and marketability of such assets by IDIC and for IDIC to certify and make affidavit about the same. In this regard, an integral part of this contract is the "Assignment Proposal (and addendum to contract)" signed and dated by the bank and acknowledged by IDIC (attached hereto). IDIC's control of such assets is on behalf of the bank's depositors. The bank acknowledges that it gives over all rights, title and interest of the required assets to IDIC via general power of attorney; and the general power of attorney by any actual owner of such assets. Further, the bank acknowledges, in the event of a legitimate claim by a depositor or depositors, that IDIC may sell or assign such assets in order to satisfy legitimate claims made by depositor(s). Any return of deposits shall include interest accrued to the date of any such settlement. While IDIC acknowledges a reinsurance contract with Standard Surety and Guaranty Corporation, said reinsurance contract is for the purpose of indemnifying IDIC against any liability to itself, or losses to its own assets incurred in the process of settling claim(s) to any depositor. Said reinsurance does not accrue coverage or interest to the bank."

All very comforting—or it would have been had the bank any legitimate assets to be realised and if IDIC had actually existed except as a figment of the imagination of Ziegler and Ferguson. The contract continued:

"The assets must exceed a ratio of $3 for every $1 on deposit. This ratio is based on a 12-month forward projection that indicates deposit trends over the previous 12 months. This projection must indicate that there are adequate assets turned over to the control of IDIC that will still exceed deposits by a 3-to-1 ratio at the end of 12 months from the date of projection. This projection will be updated each month so those assets are always at the 3 to 1 ratio for the ensuing 12 months."

Having set up a mechanism for proving to the gullible that investing in the bank posed absolutely no risk, they then went on to create The World Investment Stock Exchange, WISE, a Grenadian paper entity, dreamed up by Charles Webb, an old associate from Maui and run by a young Ziegler appointee, Mark Kennedy. Kennedy had previously been a microwave antenna installer in Canada, taken to religion in a big way following his divorce and had fallen for Ziegler's evangelical zeal after being introduced to him by the CEO of Cambridge International Trust, an FIBG correspondent bank. He was invited to come to Grenada to join the team engaged in God's work. Feeling that this might enable him to climb to even greater heights than he had so far reached in the antenna business, he accepted. One evening, walking on the silky sands of the island beaches, Ziegler confided that he had had a vision from God that Mark was destined to become the head of WISE, First Bank's own stock exchange. It is pretty indicative of Kennedy's intelligence and general thinking that he fell for it and took the job, moving into a palatial house in the hills overlooking St. Georges on the strength of the appointment. WISE was once again an IBC that offered clients of the bank the opportunity to invest in sundry exotic offerings that appeared nowhere else on the stock markets of the world. Once again, the comfort level for the investor was raised to 100% by having the value of stocks guaranteed by the bank under a scheme labeled Stock Value Bank Guarantee.

Unlike a typical stock exchange where investors buy individual shares that are not guaranteed to retain their value, investors in WISE could buy shares whose principal and interest were totally guaranteed by a Stock Value Bank Guarantee (SVBG), an instrument provided by First Bank. "A percentage of every share sold on WISE is set aside in a deposit-insured bank to guarantee a return of principal and reasonable earnings," WISE documents said. A three-year SVBG guaranteed that the investor would be returned 119% of the original investment, while the five-year SVBG guaranteed 135% and the 10-year SVBG guaranteed 211%. Approximately twelve obscure companies were listed on the exchange including a "photography and portrait studio in the Philippines." Significantly, as it proved later, another was a luxury hotel and country club on Lake Victoria in Uganda.

No investor seems to have questioned the feasibility of such an operation—and the stage was set for the sales pitch of all time.

"There are more fools in the world than there are people."

—Heinrich Heine (1797–1856)

6

A New Man

By this time, the world was taking some notice of Fidelity International Bank in distant Nauru, largely on account of the enormous interest rates that it seemed to be able to pay, an ability that baffled more conventional banks. A few depositors were receiving returns on their investments when they demanded them firmly enough, good publicity for further punters to throw in their cash. Slightly alarming though was the fact that the world was also taking some interest in the activities of its founder, Gilbert Allen Ziegler. Although a Passport carrying citizen of Melchizedek (having paid his dues to that mighty dominion), in view of the international community's unfortunate scepticism regarding its validity, this was hardly the ideal nationality for the role of international banker, and the Grenadian Economic Citizenship Programme developed by the Barnabe and Springer team seemed to be the answer, particularly as Ziegler was now part of Granite Registry Services who, helpfully, were the approved agents for the programme. Theoretically, it did not come without a hefty price tag, the official schedule calling for US$22,000 to be paid directly to the treasury and a further US$17,000 to a Government Approved project while the agent's fees added another $11,000. How much Ziegler actually coughed up is not known, but given his previous financial finagling with the government and his connection with Granite Registry and Barnabe, it seems likely that he was able to negotiate a bargain. However the name of Gilbert Ziegler was becoming a little too familiar to the regulatory authorities of the world and the new passport would seem better with a different name in it, he felt. Meditating over a few Pina Coladas on the beach, a name came to him—Van Brink. Unkind cynics later claimed that it was not so much a name that sprang from meditation but far more likely a cerebral connection with Brink's Vans, noted for their ability to cart the stuff around that FIBG aimed to collect. Be that as it may, Van Arthur Brink (his middle name also having been changed) was now a citizen of the beautiful and conveniently sloppily regulated

Islands of Grenada and the former bankrupt Gilbert Ziegler but a distant memory. Now a whole new vista opened up before him.

One bugaboo of offshore banking is that onshore governments are highly sceptical of the motives of their citizens that wish to move their money out of the grasp of their authority and, in consequence, take a dim view of attempts by the aforesaid banks to promote their wares to the general public. In other words, getting out the good news about your offshore bank's startling advantages takes a bit of cunning.

FIBG must have seemed to the unwary an incredible bargain offering returns on Certificates of Deposit of over 200% in some cases, totally risk free, and wonderful returns on stock investments through WISE, equally guaranteed to be loss free, thanks to the backing from the bank which was in itself guaranteed by an organisation as impressively named as International Deposit Insurance Corporation. Few bothered to check the credentials of any of these entities while the glitter of gold be-dazzled them. It hardly seemed worthwhile to the attendees of "wealth seminars" promoted by a clearly altruistic bunch of speakers and packed with satisfied clients.

Once again the team of Barnabe and Springer were harnessed to carry out marketing through FIBG's hastily incorporated subsidiaries Life Offshore, the Offshore Educational Institute, Granite Registry Services, and the Asset Research & Development Association. They made initial contact by giving away subscriptions to the Life Offshore newsletter, an idea that hearkened back to Van Brink's early days in Oregon. Through the Offshore Educational Institute they held seminars proclaiming the benefits of investing through FIBG and distributed promotional material through the Asset Research & Development Association. They also offered to register offshore business companies for investors through Granite Registry Services, giving them an almost impermeable umbrella against the predatory taxman.

But most convincingly of all, at the seminars potential clients were introduced to existing investors who were excited with the returns they were getting and enthusiastically recruited new members. Some of these "investors" were FIBG's agents as had been the case with Fidelity's promotions, a Mabel Bastienne from Maui being a frequent and talented performer in this role, but others, who had actually seen some returns, were encouraged by a generous commission structure offered for each new client enrolled.

And so, in April 1998, the first of the avalanche of funds started to flow into the bank. A new board of directors was appointed by Van Brink, authorised to do so by the original cast, and consisted of Van Brink as chairman and CEO, Rita

Regale as Chief Financial Officer, apparently without the benefit of any prior qualification, Marion Suite, a newly qualified Grenadian attorney who was acting for the bank, Dusean Berkirch, whose name barely surfaces subsequently and Richard Downes, an old acquaintance from Oregon. Advisors were Robert Skirving, also an old partner from the northwest and Harvey R. Kaufman.

Maintaining his policy of keeping things pretty much at arm's length, the only shareholder of the bank was a Nevis Trust, the Covenant Trust, and the sole beneficiary of the trust was Tai Hastey, now no longer a director of the bank but presumably well under Brink's control and maybe his roof also.

Will Rogers once remarked that he was not so much concerned with the return on his investment but more with the return of his investment, an attitude that barely seemed to concern the clients of the new bank who rubbed their hands at the thought of being such sharp fellows as to be able to garner incredible returns, apparently risk free, when the common lot were stuck with a few miserly percent from traditional banks. The products on offer were mainly in the form of Certificates of Deposit with returns, 100% guaranteed, thanks to IDIC, of 150% to 200% per annum. It was pointed out tactfully that these splendid results were only achieved by the bank having an asset base of $13.8 billion, an amount that would put it in the ranks of the world's biggest banks, after less than a year in business. The unlikelihood of such being the case barely seems to have registered with the depositors.

At the other end of the scale, there was the bank's problem that, having promised such returns, how to achieve them? Or appear to be able to achieve them?

As anyone with an ounce of investment savvy understands, there is absolutely no way to guarantee such huge returns or, for that matter, any returns at all. The investment business does not work like that; it is an uncertain science at best, more of an art form, and not to be relied upon to provide a steady income. However, many years before Van Brink, a Mr. Charles Ponzi had solved the immediate problem for his programme very handily by paying off early investors out of the funds received from new investors, and thus brought a new word into the English vocabulary—Ponzi. Unless you are a true believer in perpetual motion or similar devices, there is a pretty obvious catch to this system—unless you can keep the money rolling in, sooner or later things will get very difficult for you. And eventually you run out of new business and things come to a dead stop. Then it's time to leave town.

There were sporadic attempts made to place funds in something tangible. Investing in a luxury yacht does not often come within the purview of a bank's investment portfolio except by default. In the case of FIBG it was different, it was to be by design.

In May 1999, a group approached George Pearce, a retired businessman living in Nanaimo, Canada, who said they were interested in buying his yacht, a 114-foot vessel that he had recently put up for sale. Pearce met with Vancouver resident Richard Downes and two other men who claimed to be doing work for a company run by Downes. After a quick tour of the vessel—and a moment of prayer during which Downes and his companions joined hands—they offered the full asking price of $5 million. Which was fine, except they wanted to pay only $400,000 in cash. The remaining $4.6-million was to be paid in the form of a certificate of deposit from First Bank of Grenada, a bank of which Pearce had never heard.

"They said the bank had money at CIBC and a bank in Japan," he said. Pearce, who having run a successful business as a bailiff, was not the sort who was prepared to accept the statements of total strangers at face value. He decided to check them out. "Downes said he was a director of the bank and that they had this insurance on all deposits with a company called IDIC. But I checked it out and no one had ever heard of them. I was on the phone for hours with the Japanese bank. They didn't know anything about it either. So I told them that, but they just said, 'No, you're wrong, you've made a mistake.'"

Now frustrated that Pearce was clearly not going to part with his boat on their terms, Downes moved on to more familiar ground. Pearce recalls that he launched into an aggressive pitch for First Bank, trying to get him to put some money into what they called a high-yield deposit. "They said it was an offshore bank and they couldn't talk about it in Canada, it was against the law, so they wanted to fly me down to Grenada. Offered to put me up at a hotel, all expenses paid, so I could listen to an investment seminar. I heard later that they were saying that to all kinds of people." He turned them down, a decision many others were later to wish they had made.

Traditional banks employ teams of experienced investment analysts to place client funds where they will be accessible if need be and will generate a reasonable return at the same time. The FIBG team had no such experience and, as it later transpired, made no attempt to invest in anything other than Van Brink's future and two or three unlikely private ventures, all of which lost money. But even the most blasé of their lucky clients needed some explanation as to how such a new bank could generate returns that escaped the more staid institutions that had been around for a couple of hundred years. And for this, FIBG had the answer.

"A fool and his money are soon parted."

**—from Thomas Tusser's Five Hundred Points of Good
Husbandry.**

7

An Investment Programme for Those Who Believe in the Tooth Fairy—Bank Trading Debentures

Who the unsung genius was that came up with this moneymaking scheme will probably never be known. Which is a pity in a way, since in the annals of consumer fraud his name would undoubtedly have been writ large. Its success must be judged from the fact that, many years after its inception, in spite of repeated warnings from government bodies, genuine investment advisors, legitimate banks and from its many victims, like the Mississippi river it still keeps rolling along and carrying its victims to disaster.

Perhaps its enduring appeal lies in the degree of confidentiality necessarily imposed on its participants, as though they are privy to a bit of information others don't have, an inside track on the world banking system so to speak. The privileged few are adjured not to discuss the scheme for fear of letting everybody in on the secret and the anti-establishment crowd are pleased to hear that this is something that "they" don't wish to become widely known.

In essence, and there are many variations on a theme, it alleges that there is a little known ploy by the world's top banks to transfer funds and various bond instruments, letters of credit, debt instruments and the like between themselves almost on a daily basis to balance the books. By providing the large amounts of capital to fund such transfers or purchases of instruments (the sums are purportedly enormous) incredible profits can be generated for those lucky enough to be in the know, a very exclusive club. Unfortunately, the minimum amount usually quoted for an entry level into this exclusive club is around US$10 million, a figure that puts it out of reach for the average Joe Blow. Promoters of the scheme can help you out here, however. By pooling the resources of many they can accumulate the $10M and then all you need to do is to sit back and wait for the monthly payout. Sadly, it may be a very long wait.

Whilst waiting, expectant punters are cautioned not to ask too many questions for fear of upsetting the status quo and in any event, they will have signed a "non-disclosure" form couched in suitably threatening language, "under pain of perjury", (since the average person probably perjures himself more or less unwittingly, several times a week, realistically this should alarm few) plus a few other spurious documents usually bearing the insignia of the International Chamber of Commerce.

For an up and coming institution such as FIBG, it seemed that such a programme could well be presented as the source of the enormous profits allegedly being generated by the bank. Adolf Hitler once remarked that the bigger the lie, the better chance was there of the people believing it. And Van Brink and his cronies had brought lying to a new level of artistic endeavour. In a variation of the Bank Debenture programme as this was commonly referred to, FIBG claimed that, due to its access to the inner sanctum of banking and its huge asset base, it could buy debt instruments, such as bonds or letters of credit, from banks at a deep discount and redeem them at face value, profiting on the difference. The promotional literature trumpeted, "It's that simple, Buy Low, Sell High". How they were able to redeem or sell them when the issuing bank could not was never explained. Subsequent audits of the bank were to prove that no such trading was ever even attempted—but depositors swallowed the big lie, hook, line and sinker.

In terms of income, The First International Bank of Grenada was beginning to look prosperous. The sales pitches from seminars were reeling in the clients and, to prove the attractiveness of being established offshore, some meetings were now being held in Grenada at the Rex Hotel. There the lucky attendees were calmed by the lapping waters of the Caribbean, plied with frequent exotic tropical drinks and seduced by the silver tongued charm of Van Brink and Co., not infrequently aided by members of the government who provided an air of verismilitude to the whole charade. Speaking alongside a dubious cast of characters such as Larry Barnabe, David Springer, JeRu Hall and Taansen Sumeru were Grenada's Minister of Foreign Affairs, Mark Isaac; Former Registrar of Companies Robert Branch; and attorney Teddy St. Louis, whose law firm had provided services to several dubious investment firms in Grenada.

An amateurish promotional video for the bank shot at one of these meetings and now in the hands of the FBI showed Van Brink diffidently explaining how anyone can get rich by investing in offshore companies. He says he believes God meant us all to have the kind of freedom that comes with wealth. He briefly mentions investment opportunities but seems to focus mostly on how quickly believers can become rich thanks to the various wonderfully high interest rates offered by his bank. He calls the people in the audience 'friends' and looks decidedly uncomfortable at particularly dubious points, such as the part where he explains how depositors are fully protected by a company called the International Deposit Insurance Corporation. He seems to be on uncertain ground and hesitant when he is talking about banking.

As he moves on to more familiar territory, such as his personal goals and dreams, his manner becomes more positive. His object in life, he declares with a winning smile, is to help other God-fearing members of the middle class—the "little guys," he calls them—sever the bonds of financial necessity that blight their lives. It is back to his preaching days but the God he now espouses is Mammon. Some of the IC's, the commissioned sales people packing the audience, were more blunt about it, saying the government and banks conspired to keep good Christians poor, a sentiment that struck responsive chords among the newcomers to the meeting.

Having conned the government of Grenada into allowing him to operate a bank with far less than the prescribed capital requirements, unless you accept that photocopies of various assignments of nebulous assets constitute legal tender, Van Brink felt that expansion was in order.

If one phony bank can get so many suckers, half a dozen should prove a bonanza it was felt and, judging from the experience of Mr. Ponzi, it would be essential to keep the pot boiling to stave off the inevitable for as long as possible. By this time it seems that Prime Minister Mitchell was heavily indebted to FIBG. Elections were coming up and a grateful Van Brink offered to bankroll some of the expense—at a price. The deal, involving the registrar, Michael Creft, allowed FIBG to establish a number of sub-banks, all under the umbrella of First Bank and thus not having to comply with anything much in the way of capital requirements or regulatory paperwork. Eventually, FIBG and its associated banks, referred to quite erroneously as correspondent banks, would account for the large part of Grenada's offshore banking industry. All were effectively controlled and managed by the mother bank and all funds received were eventually placed in institutions controlled by FIBG but, once again, they provided an arm's length relationship, a safety net against the slings and arrows of outraged depositors. Nominee managers were appointed who were little more than salesmen for the spurious investments, none of whom appear to have had any banking qualifications for the posts. In the end no fewer than 18 banks were operating in Grenada under the aegis of The First International Bank of Grenada, all enthusiastically promoting their services to eager audiences in North America and around the world.

All in all, 1998 seemed to have been a pretty good first year for the bank and the deposit base had reached unbelievable proportions for a newly founded institution. In accordance with the rules and regulations connected with their licence, on the 9th.of September, somewhat belatedly, an auditor was appointed. Customarily a bank will have as auditors, a company from a recognised international group and one moreover, that would have been involved from the earliest days of operation. But FIBG elected to appoint a local company, Wilson and Co., to perform the service. This was a small accounting firm established in 1992 that was also involved in company management. It may have been thought that, by employing a well known Grenadian, the audit would be a mere token inspection, not too many questions asked and certainly no forensic examination of the basis of the bank's assets or of its claimed deposits. They could not have been more wrong.

By the beginning of September, the reputed asset base of FIBG consisted of the following:

An assignment of a red ruby consisting of a photocopy of an appraisal of "Boy on a Water Buffalo" valued at $20M. This was assigned to FIBG (then Fidelity Bank) in 1997 from a Nevada company called Resource Enhancement, apparently gratuitously, for there is no record of any money changing hands. It was re-assigned back to Resource Enhancement a year later in September 1998 but continued to be listed in the books of the bank as an asset.

Various cheques and instruments (all photocopies) from The Bank of China, Bank of Taiwan, Dai-Ichi Kango Bank (these were bearer cheques in the trivial amount of $3.8 Billion!), Tokyo Mitsubishi Bank and a gold certificate from The Union Bank of Switzerland, none of which were verifiable let alone cashable. Exotic additions to these traditional securities were pre-Ming Dynasty vases and various Egyptian antiquities.

All in all, a grand total of $13.89 billion—but practically nothing in liquid cash.

Wilson and Co. set to work to provide an audit to acceptable accounting standards but by December 1998, they called for a meeting with Van Brink and his unqualified Chief Financial Officer, Rita Regale, to ask a few pertinent questions concerning the bank's operations. It must have been an interesting meeting. Even a local accountant, called upon to audit a bank, might be somewhat non-plussed to be presented with a set of photocopies as evidence of their financial standing and this seemed to be the reaction of Wilson who expressed some astonishment that a bank, formed early in that year with a mere $110,000 cash deposit, suddenly claimed to have an asset base of nearly $14 billion. In general, accountants tend to lack imagination and clearly such a quantum leap was beyond the ability of Wilson and Co. to grasp. The staggering growth of the bank's deposits in so short a time seemed to elude a rational explanation. Within nine months, in its financial report to Grenadian regulators, the bank claimed it not only had the ruby and assorted *bric à brac* as collateral but also had assets under management of about US$13.8 billion as of 31 December 1998.

Unhappy and dissatisfied with the meeting they retired to their offices across the harbour on Lagoon Road and re-considered their position. Van Brink and Tai Hastey had a Merry Chistmas in the house at Morne Rouge, Point Saline on the southwest corner of Grenada, purchased by the bank for them.

But the wheels were already coming off the wagon.

"Oh what a tangled web we weave,
When first we practise to deceive!"

—**Sir Walter Scott (1771–1832)**

8

Trouble in Paradise

Nevis is a delightful island, almost a paradise in fact. Not over populated, with friendly and intelligent locals, little crime and an enviable life style, it does however lack much in the way of industry and, as with other islands, offshore business was the main money-spinner. As we pointed out before, with a population of only ten thousand, regulating such an industry was virtually impossible and consequently Nevis became the destination of choice for a number of less than reputable operators. Main Street, Charlestown is the major thoroughfare through town but it would be possible to chuck a rock down its entire length. It does house an incredible number of offshore companies in that short distance and in one of these multi-faceted office buildings, The Heritage Plaza, was housed The International Deposit Insurance Corporation. Or, more accurately, the company documents of this impressively named institution were housed there, since the company had no physical presence and resided solely in the files of its Registered Agent and in the minds of its principal, Douglas Ferguson and of its creator, Van Brink.

Several hundred miles to the north in Miami sat an investigative reporter, David Marchant, whose writings had already been giving severe heartburn to many of the financial scamsters operating in the offshore field. His monthly publication, Offshore Alert, although with a scanty subscription list due to a hefty price tag of around $60 a copy, was widely read by professionals in the financial services sector. Always on the lookout for a good story, Marchant became intrigued with a company claiming to act as an insurer, clearly without a licence, in a jurisdiction that was already under his personal microscope as a hotbed of dodgy corporations. IDIC looked interesting and he started to make some probing enquiries. The very name was suggestive of shady practice, being suspiciously akin to FDIC, and soon a link to a new offshore bank became apparent. That this should be in Grenada, another suspect island, merely increased his curiosity and, aided by some queries from outside, he fired up a campaign of enquiry. Bald, bold and belligerent by nature, Marchant started kicking up some dust in the IDIC area and, soon enough, the Nevis authorities saw fit to enquire of IDIC just what was going on.

Douglas Ferguson's answers to their questions were lengthy, evasive and, to the head of the financial service authority in Nevis, Mr. Laurie Lawrence, far from satisfactory. Six days later he wrote back to Ferguson:

> *"Your letter failed to give us the desired assurances regarding the questions that were raised in our original correspondence. This fact has fortified in our minds that your operation must be closed down as a matter of urgency. The facts which led to this decision, and of which you are already aware are as follows:*
>
> 1. *The advertising of International Depositors' Reinsurance Corporation and the manner in which you are conducting your business raises serious regulatory considerations.*
>
> 2. *By your own account, International Depositors' Reinsurance Corporation is not governed by any jurisdiction, nor regulated by any jurisdiction.*
>
> 3. *International Depositors' Reinsurance Corporation is not licensed by the Nevis Island Administration to conduct business of any kind in Nevis.*
>
> 4. *International Depositor's Reinsurance Corporation has been doing business as International Depositor's Insurance Corporation and has been operating and passing itself off as an insurance company in Nevis licensed to offer services to non-residents.*
>
> *Take notice that you are required to close and cease all operations in Nevis with immediate effect. Any failure by you to cease operations will result in such legal action as the Nevis Island Administration deems appropriate in the circumstances."*

Ferguson took the hint, bundled up the few files the company had, not too big a problem since FIBG was their sole customer, and decamped for a friendlier clime. The hiatus this caused in the telephone services was passed off as being "due to an upgrade" but when normal service came to be resumed, the numbers were those of an attorney's office, one Gerald Burton, in Dominica.

But the troubles of IDIC were merely the tip of an iceberg and the good ship FIBG was heading firmly that way like a financial Titanic. With the tenacity of a terrier after a particularly juicy specimen of rat, David Marchant homed in, not only on IDIC but FIBG, WISE and the old Fidelity Bank in Nauru. His New Year present to Van Brink was to publish details of these operations in the January edition of Offshore Alert with clear warnings that all of these entities were likely to be fraudulent. Panicking, Van Brink got together with a compliant Michael Creft and persuaded him to write to Marchant complaining of the allegations and refuting them absolutely, at the same time expressing surprise that Nevis had acted so immoderately in regard to IDIC. Dutifully, Creft gave FIBG and its associated companies a clean bill of health and in a letter, warned Marchant against spreading unsubstantiated rumours.

Things were not going too smoothly in the relationship with the auditors either. Attempting to establish the bona fides of the bits of paper they had been presented with as assets, Wilson and Co. not unreasonably wished to have something a little more substantial than the word of Van Brink to attest to their value. Now they were to find that, in most cases, FIBG did not even have the listed assets, they had only been assigned to FIBG from a company in The Bahamas, Sherwood Investments. Sherwood Investments proved to be nothing more than a shell company set up by Brink associates. Van Brink then said they should go to an unspecified destination in the United States to inspect the supporting documents, to which Lauriston Wilson replied that it would surely be easier for the documents to come to Grenada, where, as listed assets of the bank, they should have been in the first place. Suggesting that it might be easier if they contacted the issuing banks directly, they were rebuffed in a faxed letter from Brink on the 24th. February:

> *"As I explained to you in our last telephone conversation, the instruments we hold are not in the name of First International Bank of Grenada. They were issued to other parties; First Bank received them by way of deed of assignment. You have photocopies of all of these instruments and of the Deeds of Assignment with clearly referenced confirmation coordinates.*
>
> *The transfers via Deed of Assignment can be confirmed directly by your firm writing the party which made the assignment and faxing to the coordinates given. All such confirmation will be made by an attorney who could well be described as the "Who" in Who's Who of attorneys in British Columbia. Moreover, the assigments of certain instruments have come with a lengthy affidavit concerning authentication which took place all the way back to the Finance minister of Japan.*
>
> *Your office has no authority to communicate directly with the original issuing banks, as such would not be acknowledged with them unless we were to pay a re-issue fee and a confirmation fee as relates to each instrument. In the case of those instruments valued in the billions of dollars, such re-issue and confirmation fees would start at about USD$10 million. Your firm should be capable of confirming the assigments by way of direct correspondence with the assigning party, together with certification by the law firm which coordinated the assignments."*

Apparently unimpressed by the reference to an entry in Who's Who of Attorneys for British Columbia, Wilson and Co. called it quits and prepared to resign as auditors of the bank.

9

More Paper for The Government

Van Brink was concerned. Offshore Alert might have few readers but the few they had tended to be influential and the intransigent Nevis attitude over IDIC was alarming. Mindful of his previous successes in bamboozling Grenada with fraudulent paper, he came up with the idea of publicly offering a substantial bond to the government as a token of good faith. Naturally the bond would be purely on paper and, even more frugally, would only pledge some of the forged paper items already listed as assets of the bank. To ensure that the announcement would appear more legitimate, he arranged that it should be made as a Press Release from WISE:

For Immediate Release: February 16, 1999

FIRST BANK POSTING FINANCIAL GUARANTEE WITH GOVERNMENT

St. George's, Grenada—First International Bank of Grenada, Limited ("First Bank") is posting a financial guarantee with the Government of Grenada in the amount of $50 million USD as a demonstration of its good faith and financial integrity in dealings with its non-Grenadian depositors, according to (Miss) Marion Suite, legal counsel for First Bank, adding that by law "offshore" banks, such as First Bank, are not allowed to take deposits from Grenadian citizens. First Bank's unprecedented initiative of providing proof of its financial capability is one element in a larger strategy to put to rest all questions concerning its credibility as Grenada's largest offshore bank and employer of approximately thirty Grenadians.

Suite explained that the idea to volunteer such a financial guarantee was suggested in an informal meeting of the bank's directors who were discussing an article appearing in the January 29th issue of Offshore Alert, an Internet quasi-newsletter service, which alleged that First Bank was a fraud.

"If it wasn't that some people will no doubt take the Offshore Alert article seriously, we would all just have something to laugh about over lunch," Suite said,

57

noting that among other things the editors of the article attacking First Bank wrote that the fact that First Bank paid its depositors the interest due proved that First Bank was operating an illegal Ponzi scheme. "What are we to infer from this," Suite asked, "that in order to be regarded as legitimate, a bank must default on its obligations to depositors? What kind of logic are they using?"

Suite made it clear that First Bank takes attacks on its credibility seriously and is having a Florida law firm prepare a suit for USD $100 million in damages against a Mr. David Marchant and the Florida-based Offshore Alert Internet journal. "The article was filled with deliberate lies, innuendoes, unsubstantiated allegations and misleading statements, all in the pretext of 'exposing' First Bank as a fraud preying upon unsuspecting residents of the United States, Canada, and Germany," Suite said, noting that the bank was confident of winning judgment against Marchant and Offshore Alert.

According to documents filed with the government's Offshore Financial Services Division, First Bank has grown to almost USD $50 million in deposits, while at the same time growing to just under USD $14 billion in total capital and retained earnings, Suite said.

Suite noted that the word "fraud" in financial dealings connotes an institution of no genuine substance passing itself off as having genuine financial substance and ability. In banking, she said this would amount to a bank having an overwhelming lack of capital in the face of its obligations to depositors and other creditors. "But when you have a bank capitalized and operating at nearly three hundred times the amount of its total liabilities, the only 'fraud' would be in calling such a bank a fraud," Suite said.

Also alleged to be fraudulent in the Offshore Alert article was the Nevis-based International Depositors' Reinsurance Corporation ("IDIC"), Ltd., the third-party administrator of First Bank's self-insurance program which guarantees all depositors their capital invested and any interest due.

Suite explained that under the IDIC system, each participating bank must have assets under IDIC control that more than covers the bank's deposits. The ratio of IDIC-available assets to cash deposits determines IDIC's rating of a participating bank. A ratio of 1:1 equates to a "C" rating; a ratio of 2:1 equates to a "B" rating; a ratio of 3:1 equates to an "A" rating; a ratio of 5:1 equates to an "AA" rating; and a ratio of 10:1 equates to an "AAA" rating. First Bank has maintained a rating of "AAA" since it was organized and licensed in Grenada in October 1997.

According to the Offshore Alert article, when Marchant told the Nevis Island Administration that he was running an exposé on IDIC, naming it as part of a scam involving First Bank and the bank's preying upon unsuspecting depositors, the Nevis Island Administration moved to immediately close IDIC's Nevis office.

"It appears that Marchant was successful in scaring Nevis with his yellow-journalism tactics in Offshore Alert," Suite said, noting that IDIC has since filed an action in the High Court of Justice against Hon. Vance Amory, Nevis Minister of Finance; The Nevis Island Administration; Laurie Lawrence, Permanent Secretary, Ministry of Finance; Agatha Jeffers-Gooden, Director, Financial Services

Department; and the Attorney General of the Federation of St. Christopher and Nevis, for breach of contract on the part of Nevis and for acting contrary to Nevis law and without due process of law. IDIC expects that there will be quick resolution in the matter at a hearing to be held within the next few weeks.

In keeping with the tone being set by IDIC, Suite indicated that First Bank would take legal action against anyone making unsubstantiated and damaging statements about its operations.

"The important thing to First Bank is that its depositors can rest assured that their deposits are absolutely safe, which is why First Bank is posting the USD $50 million financial guarantee with the Government of Grenada," Suite said. "Then it's back to banking business as usual, leaving the courts to decide who's fraudulent, and who's not."

Meanwhile, Suite reported that there had been repeated attempts on the part of Mr. David Marchant of Offshore Alert to have First Bank's license revoked by the Government of Grenada. In response to the allegations presented by Offshore Alert, Grenada's Offshore Financial Services Department has performed an investigation, taking statements from all the Grenada parties named by Offshore Alert and reviewing various official and private documents that totally refute the allegations made. "There is no substantiation of the allegations made and no verifiable reports of wrong doing on the part of First Bank or by its employees, officers and directors," Suite said.

Quoting from First Bank's copy of a letter written by the Offshore Financial Services office in response to Marchant's repeated attempts to have First Bank's license revoked, she said, "Grenada's offshore sector is governed by the laws thoughtfully enacted by its Parliament and administered by its government. These laws are designed to protect the public, to safeguard the reputation of Grenada, and to defend the lawful activities of those companies which are lawfully established."

With respect to First Bank, the letter affirmed that the First Bank well exceeded the capital requirements at its formation and that it does so to this date. It also noted that the Offshore Financial Services office has received not one substantiated complaint concerning First Bank's operations.

"Grenada does not operate its offshore sector by hear-say, innuendo and unsubstantiated allegations," Suite said, adding that "First Bank did not receive its license on that basis, nor will Grenada law permit First Bank to lose its license on that basis. First Bank was legally established in Grenada and has demonstrated that it operates wholly within the law in its banking activities," Suite said.

When asked why First Bank became targeted by Offshore Alert, Suite said it was unclear, but that there had been unsubstantiated reports that a competitor offshore bank had complained about the high interest rates First Bank pays its offshore banking clientele, even to the point of filing a complaint with the FBI in the United States.

"It seems that there is a lot of jealousy among some of the offshore banks over how well First Bank has done," Suite said. "Rather than face the friendly competition offered by First Bank, it seems that these isolated bankers would resort to *underhanded tactics, complete with bogus complaints filed with legal authorities and false stories planted in the press."*

Suite also pointed out that successful offshore banks are often the target of unfriendly, speculative press. "Many people think that nothing good could come from offshore banks," she said, adding that banking and government regulators from the larger nations try to keep that myth alive to discourage their citizens from investing money in other countries.

By offering the $50 million financial guarantee to the Government of Grenada, Suite said First Bank is sending a simple message to its offshore banking competitors—"Put up or shut up."

Suite stated that to date no other Grenada offshore bank has put up a financial guarantee to the government to demonstrate the safety of financial operations. "Financial guarantees are not required by law," she explained, noting that evidence of verifiable, documented financial capability was sufficient to meet the requirements of Grenada's offshore banking laws. Such a requirement is the same as in those other jurisdictions offering offshore sector banking. Suite also noted that no request for the financial guarantee had been made by the government, but that it was entirely the suggestion and the volunteered offering of First Bank.

Also accused by Offshore Alert as being part of a conspiracy of fraud against American and Canadian investors, was the Grenadian-based World Investors Stock Exchange ("WISE"), a company that offers an Internet listing service for sales of stock.

The business plan of WISE is to assist in the selling of shares in various listed international business companies, only insofar as those shares are backed by a bank guarantee issued by First Bank.

"First Bank has demonstrated to us that it does have the financial substance to write such guarantees," Suite said, noting that First Bank also has the license to issue its bank guarantees. "There is no law in Grenada that WISE violates by insisting that share sales it coordinates be backed by a guarantee by a financially-capable, licensed banking institution. How Offshore Alert has concluded this to be fraud remains a mystery to my clients," she added.

"There are many interesting assertions made by Offshore Alert", WISE's president, Mark Kennedy commented. "So far as I can tell, none of the negative allegations are true. But, at least, he spelled the companies names correctly," he added.

One of the allegations made by Offshore Alert was that WISE's parent company, a Covenant Trust, Ltd., of Nevis was struck off the Nevis registry in August 1998. "This statement is a total variance with the facts," Kennedy said, showing documents that affirmed that the annual fees required of Covenant Trust had been paid in July 1998, and producing a Certificate of Good Standing issued by the Nevis Island Administration on behalf of Covenant Trust, Ltd.

Suite's final comment was one of high praise for the effectiveness of Grenada's Offshore Financial Services Division office. "One thing is certain," she said, "should any party present the Government of Grenada with any real evidence of fraud or misconduct on the part of any offshore company which his office licenses and regulates, it would be expeditiously investigated and promptly acted upon."

But in the event that negative allegations bear no provable substance, she expressed her confidence that the government will justly support the companies licensed and regulated under Grenada law. "Reckless smear campaigns hurt not only offshore companies, but also the Government and the people of Grenada and cast aspersions on the integrity of our jurisdiction," she said.

Ms. Suite, who appeared to be in some confusion as to her role, being a director of First Bank but not of WISE for whom she was now acting as spokeswoman, did not bother to explain her role or how she came to be able to quote, verbatim, from a letter from a government department to a private citizen in the United States.

The bond for $50,000,000 was duly typed up on First Bank letterheading assigning the two worthless Bank of China Guarantees with a face value of $25 million each, to be held as surety against any malfeasance by the bank. Signed by Brink and Regale, the letters were stamped "received" by Michael Creft's office.

Across the harbour, Wilson's office noted the developments with some concern. They had been totally frustrated in their efforts to conduct an audit on the bank, ledgers were not available, records were incomplete, the officers evasive and Wilson could find no trace of any legitimate assets in spite of the lofty claims being made. Even more alarming was a letter received from Van Brink on First Bank letterheading:

I would appreciate it if you could inquire of Grenada Co-Operative Bank as to what is the limit of their ability to receive a wire of U.S. Dollars in the following amounts:

*$500,000
*$1,000,000
*$5,000,000
*$10,000,000
*$25,000,000
*$50,000,000
*$100,000,000
*$500,000,000
*$1,000,000,000
*No limit

The mere mention of such sums immediately raised the spectre of a possible money laundering operation in his own backyard.

Thoughtfully he mulled over the situation and concluded that, before resigning their commission, some action needed to be taken.

Meanwhile Brink and Co were embarking upon a campaign of self justification and, on the 26th., Brink submitted an affidavit to the court in Grenada in support of a $100 million action against David Marchant and his company, Offshore Business News. The affidavit claimed that FIBG had $200 of equity for every $1 of deposits which, had it been correct, must have made it the strongest bank in the entire world.

"Any fool can tell the truth, but it requires a man of some sense to know how to lie well."

—**Samuel Butler (1835–1902)**

10

Gathering Thunderclouds

The rumblings in the offshore world, largely inspired by the writings of the irrepressible David Marchant, had finally reached the ears of the Prime Minister of Grenada, Dr. Keith Mitchell. Now safely re-elected, due in part to a handsome donation from FIBG to the party funds, his attention was being drawn increasingly to the fact that, as an offshore centre, Grenada was rapidly becoming about as popular as a pork-pie in a synagogue in the eyes of the legitimate banking community. Problems were growing for the entire offshore banking system worldwide as a quasi-official body in Europe, The Financial Action Task Force, FATF, attempted to reign in the taxfree delights of the offshore world. Curiously, Grenada had not yet appeared on the so-called "black list" of jurisdictions deemed to be non-cooperative in the matter of reporting tax matters, and Mitchell was clearly anxious that their interest should not be aroused. (Subsequently it was found that the omission of Grenada from the list was due only to the FATF thinking they were part of St. Vincent and The Grenadines, already black-listed, showing that geography should be required reading for anyone aspiring to membership of international committees).

Adding to his grief was the discovery that his appointee, Registrar Michael Creft, had unbelievably delegated the licensing of offshore banks and companies to Granite Registry Services, an ex-patriate company now virtually under the thumb of Brink. Unknown to him at the time, although probably suspected, was the fact that Registrar Creft was benefiting greatly from this cosy arrangement as was Creft's "significant other", in Brink's own delicate phraseology, who was now rolling around the island in a new $30,000 car, courtesy of the bank.

Taking a closer look at the situation, Mitchell realised belatedly that the apparent boom in the island's offshore banking industry revolved almost exclusively around one operation. First International Bank of Grenada might well have been renamed the Sole International Bank of Grenada, nearly every other being a mere paper satellite, feeding its income into FIBG who were entirely responsible for its incorporation, spurious funding and management.

Mindful of the painful collapse of the industry in Montserrat, he summoned Van Brink and Creft to a meeting on Saturday, March 27th. 1999. It must have been a traumatic experience for them both. In fine aggressive form, Mitchell accused them of gross violations of the banking act, apparently barely pausing for breath let alone answers. Rounding on Brink he demanded to know "why had he changed his name from Ziegler to Brink?" Rapidly according himself celebrity status, Brink replied, weakly, "in the United States, celebrities usually changed their name. There's nothing wrong in that." The Prime Minister shot back that he refused to buy that argument, having lived in the USA himself for some time and that he was well aware of the reasons why some people changed their name. Now suspicious of the background of Van Brink in view of the Offshore Alert articles and reports on possible fraudulent activity at Fidelity Bank in Nauru, he concluded that there was probably an ulterior motive for the name change. Wisely, Van Brink did not mention that, "the name came to him in a vision" but he did manage to blame the delay and failure to produce an audit for his new bank fairly and squarely on the shoulders of Wilson and Co. without expanding on the details.

At the back of the PM's mind may have been a letter Brink had written in late November, advocating in pretty strong terms that Grenada should grant the bank a 99 year lease on some land that could then be designated sovereign territory, creating, effectively, a new nation rather as The Dominion of Melchizedek had failed to do (they had been unable to come up with any suitable landmass to claim). Theoretically this would have enabled Brink and his entire crew to shelter behind a wall of diplomatic immunity although realistically the chances of such a "dominion" being recognised internationally would have been zero. The argument was as specious as it was bizarre but it was indicative of the thinking that, even now, the crew were seeking a bolthole for the inevitable day when the roof would cave in.

The interview was then terminated with the PM losing what little patience he had and telling Brink not to have any further dealings with him until he had got his act together, although quite what his meaning was in this was unclear.

Brink, no shrinking violet when it came to speaking up, later said he had barely been able to get a word in edgeways during the Prime Minister's tirade.

Creft and Brink must have left to do some serious thinking over that weekend. Meanwhile a carefully composed letter from Wilson and Co. was on its way to the Prime Minister that would produce more than a slight headache for First Bank in general and Brink and Creft in particular.

11

The Wilson Bombshell

For a small local accountancy practice, garnering an account such as First Bank's would seem to be a considerable coup. Not only would the fees be large enough to put the practice well into a comfortable profit arena but it would follow that they would also be called upon to oversee the accounts of all the ancillary banks and companies under the First's growing umbrella.

Thus it must have been with mixed feelings that Lauriston Wilson put pen to paper and crafted a carefully worded but damning letter to the Prime Minister, a Prime Minister who was already steaming from his earlier confrontation with Brink and Creft and now growing increasingly suspicious that he had been backing the wrong horse in the offshore banking stakes. Uncompromisingly the letter was headed "First International Bank of Grenada Ltd.—Violations of the Offshore Banking Act, 1996." and went on to list the lack of accounting systems and controls, lack of cooperation of the Chief Executive (Brink), lack of "forthrightness" on the part of the Chief Executive and their suspicion that the assets of the bank were bogus. Also questioned was the bank's astonishing claim that its capital had increased from $110,000 to over $14 billion in one year. According to their financial statements for March 31, 1999, First Bank held about $74 billion worth of assets on behalf of clients. But there was no way to see the actual assets the bank claimed. When Wilson asked to view the famous ruby, he was presented with a photograph and an appraisal provided by a company in Los Angeles. It was the same story with the other assets.

Brink claimed that other records had been misplaced. "We asked for names and addresses of asset holders," says Wilson. "He said no, it would cost at least ten million dollars in each case. So we said, let us approach the custodians of the assets ourselves. But that wasn't possible either. We were running into roadblocks whenever we asked for proof."

In view of his recent "fireside chat" with Brink and Creft, none of this may have come as much of a surprise to Mitchell but Wilson's next recommendation was. He suggested that the actions of the Registrar, Offshore Financial Services, were corrupt, that his demeanour betrayed a total ignorance of his duties as Registrar and that he should be sent on immediate leave to allow a thorough investigation "and cleansing" to take place in the department. Wilson added that a competent professional be appointed to take over from Creft and suggested that a Mr. Garvey Louison, a former Auditor General of Grenada, would be suitable for the post.

Rattled, Mitchell put through an urgent phone call to Wilson and asked, "Was he trying to give him a heart attack?" Wilson responded that he felt it his duty as a professional to forward the information and warned the Prime Minister against sharing information with Creft whom he emphasised once again as being corrupt. He added that Brink was trying to remove incriminating documents from their offices and Mitchell agreed that they should be retained for possible presentation to a government enquiry. However, he said he would have difficulty in removing Michael Creft as Registrar since he was regarded as a loyal party member and anyway he did not have "a smoking gun". Wilson replied that, on the contrary, he had evidence of a whole artillery battery of smoking guns and asked that they meet to review the material urgently. Twisting the knife, he pointed out the inadvisability of any political party accepting money from an offshore bank as they then felt that they could do as they pleased in the country and hold the Prime Minister to ransom. Struggling, Mitchell responded lamely that "generally he didn't know who contributed or donated money to the party", a highly unlikely circumstance, but that he "always put Grenada first in all his dealings," a statement that Wilson, who had backed the opposition party in the recent election, was unlikely to accept.

He then went on to detail Creft's delegation of the due diligence reviews of applications for Offshore Banking Licences, Trust Licences and IBC's to a locally incorporated International Business Company registered in Grenada and operated by foreigners, Granite Registry Services, pointing out that such an arrangement was highly questionable (to put it mildly) in terms of transparency, accountability and integrity. He once again warned the Prime Minister against discussing any of these matters with Creft as, "I have a strong suspicion that Creft is reporting everything to Van Brink."

To make sure that Mitchell got a true picture of the financial games being played at First Bank, Wilson then disclosed details of an offer made by Ms. Marion Suite, acting on behalf of First Bank, to pay $50 million for a recording studio in Trinidad that was in receivership. The value of the studio was reliably assessed at $12 million, which caused the offer of approximately 4.2 times the true value of the property to raise serious concerns in Trinidad as to the operations of First Bank and indeed of banks in Grenada in general. He then continued with his suspicions that FIBG was a money laundering operation.

After thirty minutes of listening to undiluted bad news, Mitchell had had enough and rang off, promising to continue the discussion at a later date.

Incredibly, nothing happened. Creft remained in place as Registrar and First Bank obtained a court order to recover their documents from Wilson and Co. Van Brink took a single-spaced, two-page advert in the weekly newspaper the Grenadian Voice in which he defended himself, denying both the auditor's findings and David Marchant's continuing allegations in Offshore Alert.

Brink asserted in the ad that he had repaid half the $1.1 million in debts from his 1994 Oregon bankruptcy and that the "precious stone" that helped capitalize the bank was worth $20 million and was a legitimate asset of the bank. He conceded that he first entered Grenada on a passport from the Dominion of Melchizedek as "ambassador at large" but asserted that the entity has a government and "sovereign claim to an above-sea-level landmass," a phrase much used in the Dominion's promotional literature.

And still the money rolled in. The seminars continued, promising offshore riches beyond the dreams of slightly more than average avarice, and one or two clients were even lucky enough to be able to collect some return on their investment.

There did remain the slight difficulty that the bank remained unaudited. Wilson and Co. had resigned in March having refused to continue with the charade but the Offshore Banking Act required, even with the connivance of a corrupt Registrar, that an audit be performed. Brink sought the services of a man who had been of help to him previously with Fidelity Bank, Kenneth Craig, CPA. Except that he was no longer a CPA, his licence having been revoked in 1996, a fact of which Van Brink, in spite of his later denials, must have been aware.

Nonetheless, on the 14th. May, Brink wrote an official letter to Creft, confirming Craig's appointment to complete the audit that Wilson had failed to accomplish. In view of the obviously cosy relationship between Van Brink and Creft, such a letter must be regarded as little more than a bureaucratic fraud to complete the formalities.

Van Brink's letter asserts that: "*Mr. Kenneth Craig is a Certified Public Accountant who practises in Nevada. Craig's Firm has over 100 years of practice associated with banks, savings and loans, credit unions, oil and gas producers, enetertainers, hospitals and other related business enterprises.*"

En route he took a sideswipe at Wilson and Co. saying, *"given the recent local tension related to a prominent St. George's accounting firm's unwillingness to prepare and present accounting reports in a customary manner (on the firm's letterhead), and due to the complexity of First Bank's financial operations and the difficulty inexperienced accountants would have in organising and presenting the bank's financial records, we felt it was best to call in an outside accounting firm that has specialised in performing bank examinations."*

He then humbly begs forgiveness for the lateness of the audit, citing the fact that they had to obtain a court order to recover the documents from Wilson, omitting the fact that the Prime Minister had asked Wilson to retain them "for a possible investigation."

By this time, Craig was already involved and had, in fact, submitted his first report on the affairs of First Bank on the 30th. May. Strangely for an accountant practising in Nevada, the report is on a letterheading bearing an address of Guanajuato, Mexico and is clearly intended to imply that an audit had been performed. Although the wording and presentation most certainly do not conform to the accepted standards for such work and was in no way shape or form, an audit, it appeared sufficient to the Registrar, Michael Creft, and First Bank continued to thrive.

12

All That Glisters
(does not always pay 125% p.a.)

To Bill and Julie, a Caribbean cruise seemed to be just what the financial doctor ordered. Both self-employed, him as a computer consultant and her as a beautician, they had managed to save a small nest egg but were undecided just where to place it to hatch. Bill felt he knew too little about the stockmarket to play there and the returns seemed uncertain. US banks were hardly likely to provide the returns on the $100,000 or so they had saved that would do much for their lifestyle and, in any case, they were concerned that the IRS might take too close an interest in the matter of their finances should they make much of it.

One of Julie's clients, under the influence of a series of mudpacks, steam baths and expensive facials, told her of a financial seminar she had attended recently in nearby Las Vegas with her husband. It had been arranged by The Offshore Educational Institute, a responsible enough sounding group. The magic word was "offshore", seemingly opening up vistas of incredibly high returns on investments with the added appeal that these appeared to be out of the reach of a grasping taxman. Although she herself was a little hazy on the details, her husband had been sufficiently impressed to make a small investment of $25,000 on which he was already receiving, in monthly payments, a return of 40% for the first year. At her next beautification session, she showed Julie a photocopy of the Certificate of Deposit they held, showing, impressively, that the bank was rated "AAA" by The International Deposit Corporation (IDIC) and bearing the slogan "Creating a More Abundant World One Beneficiary at a Time." She explained that the bank was run by a semi-religious evangelical group for the benefit of mankind in general and that the high yield payable to depositors was due to the bank having access to little known financial structures that governments in general wished to keep from their taxpayers.

Bill and Julie were interested. Both had some empathy with the church and a total antipathy for the government so the setup was doubly appealing. Bill, cautious by nature, wanted more information and was shown a rate sheet for High Yield Investment Certificates showing interest payments of up to 125% p.a. for a 5 year term. A listed feature of the CD's was that all deposits and interest were insured by IDIC for the full amount, a footnote mentioning that this was not FDIC, a US government body, which only insured amounts up to $100,000. IDIC was clearly a far superior arrangement.

Their new financial gurus pointed out that, unfortunately, due to the unreasonable attitude of the US government, the bank was not allowed to advertise on the mainland but that, by happy chance, they were arranging for a cruise to Grenada where they could meet with the principals and, if so inclined, make their deposit in person.

Bill and Julie needed a vacation and the prospect of being allowed into such a lucrative and exclusive group was exciting. They were booked on the cruise.

> *"As the trade winds rustle palms on idyllic beaches, they carry hints of spice—nutmeg, cinnamon, cloves and vanilla—enticing you to discover the Spice Island, Grenada. The Rex Grenadian commands spectacular views, across its lake and gardens, over the white sands and turquoise Caribbean waters of Tamarind Bay, towards St. George's, the island's capital."*

So runs the promotional literature of the Rex Hotel in Grenada. They might also have added that, in the case of attendees of The First International Bank of Grenada's Wealth Seminar, the trade winds also carried the rustle of dollar bills. One of the advantages to the organisers of such meetings is that tropical islands in general have a soporific effect on the fiscal acumen of normally astute people, especially if they are held at a time of year when many would have been shovelling snow from their driveways if they had stayed home. Sipping one of the free and fruity cocktails by the poolside, banking offshore seemed to equate with a dreamlike lifestyle that would be readily attainable if only you would put your trust, and your dollars, in the hands of First Bank or one of the growing number of "correspondent" banks.

So it seemed to Bill and Julie who had spent the day listening to various presentations extolling the virtues of First Bank, IDIC and WISE. Bill's concerns over the security of his investment were soon assuaged by the fortuitous and comforting presence of the Executive Director of IDIC, Mr. Douglas C. Ferguson himself, a Canadian Santa Claus of a man. In a private conversation during a break in the day's events, he was able to explain the philosophy of the insurance operation and showed him, in complete confidence he pointed out, the Membership Criteria for a client bank, emphasising that there was to be a ratio of 3 to 1 in favour of IDIC in "blocked assets" over which they held a general power of attorney, these assets having to be independently verified by IDIC's attorney, Gerald D. Burton. These "hard blocked assets" were to be liquidated if the bank defaulted and in addition, IDIC held an ex-officio position on the board of member banks that ensured that they could keep an eye on things. Ferguson showed Bill, once again "in confidence", a letter addressed "to whom it may concern" giving more details of the operation in which he stated that IDIC had independent "hard assets", a favourite phrase of his, of around $20 million. He refrained from telling him that this letter was the same one that had so signally failed to impress the regulators in Nevis. He also did not mention that IDIC had been thrown out of their latest home by the regulators in Dominica for the same reason and now had no earthly presence, only existing on a website in cyberspace.

During the meeting and at the social events that followed they had mingled, not only with their friends who had organised the trip for them, but with many other satisfied depositors, all of whom were anxious that they should also become lucky investors.

On reason for their enthusiasm was soon apparent. Most of these depositors were referred to by the bank as "IC's", Independent Contractors, employed on a commission basis to rustle up new sales. As these were, in effect, acting as unlicensed brokers in their home states, they were most certainly acting illegally, a minor point that was unlikely to concern First Bank who never even bothered to keep a true record of their identities or activities. IC's did, however, have to purchase an IBC from Granite Registry Services, generating more funds for the First Bank coffers, a purchase, which was explained as being necessary to protect their interests. More complex was the GIFT programme, the Given in Freedom Trust, located as an IBC in Nevis. Through the GIFT pyramid commission program, investors were offered the chance to earn money by referring others to FIBG. An account would be opened for them into which FIBG put US$3 and for every referral an investor made that resulted in a new account, they would receive a further 'gift' of 33 cents. For every successful referral that those brought into the scheme made, the investor would also get 33 cents, and so on down the chain. FIBG calculated that once the pyramid had reached 12 tiers, each of three referrals, the original investor would receive US$20,615.13 annually, based on the growth of the underlying 'trust' with a capital value of US$265,457.23.

This was a pure and simple pyramid selling scheme offering theoretically great returns to participants by depositing the commissions, tax-free, in a pseudo trust account.

There also seemed to be a confusing number of separate banks represented, each with their own IC's, but all offering similar programmes and claiming to be "correspondents" of First Bank

None of this was of much concern to Bill and Julie, who were only interested in earning money from their investment, being too busy to be interested in acting as sales agents. In the quiet of their room that evening, they talked it over, reviewed the extensive paperwork they had been supplied with (most of it still bearing the old Fidelity Bank logo), and agreed to go ahead. They opted for what was called The "NEWPP" Monthly Pay High Yield account, NEWPP standing for No Early Withdrawal of Principal Permitted. Their Annuity Style CD would pay them monthly and for the five year term they agreed upon, would deliver a handsome 108% per year, more than enough to cover their living expenses.

They would have preferred the "Super NEWPP" Monthly Plan but this required a minimum investment of $1,000,000, a figure way beyond them. It promised to return a comfortable 250% over five years, all fully insured of course.

Next day they met with Tai Hastey in the lobby of the hotel. Julie referred to her as "the enforcer" on account of her persuasive sales approach, but she was charming and helpful. Yes, she would be happy to accept a cheque drawn on a US bank and no, they would issue the CD without having to wait for it to clear, after all, trust was everything, wasn't it? Bill wrote a personal cheque for $100,000, Tai gave him a receipt and promised to have the CD delivered within a few hours. She felt that they should have invested in an IBC as well for their own security, however, an offer that they politely declined, feeling that the added cost was not justified.

On their way back home to Nevada, they congratulated themselves on having made such a smart move, after all, it was all insured 100%, even the interest, by that nice man from IDIC.

Sure enough, the interest payments started to arrive. A little puzzled that the cheques were actually drawn on a Nevada bank in the name of a Nevada corporation, they checked, an easy matter since they were resident locally. The company proved to be a shell company with a maildrop address. Calling the bank in Grenada, Chief Financial Officer Rita Regale explained to them that First Bank had holdings all over the world, it was just more convenient and, she hinted, more discreet to do it this way. Satisfied they thought no more of it—until their cancelled cheque for $100,000 was received from their bank. It had been deposited in The Gold Trust Bank, Kampala, Uganda.

13

The Heads of The Hydra

In Greek mythology, Heracles was sent to kill the Hydra, a many-headed snake that had the convenient ability to reproduce at will if one head was cut off. It had been a tough job but Heracles had managed it (Greek Gods usually did). In creating his banking empire Van Brink had produced a financial Hydra but lacked Heracles skill or divine assistance to be able to kill it off when needed or even to control it.

To protect First Bank and himself from possible confrontation with enraged depositors, the correspondent bank setup had been devised. By allowing selected clients to form their own bank, deposits into which would be indirectly handled and controlled by First Bank, a firewall would be created, any malfeasance being directly attributable to the unfortunate correspondent bank and its owner. Thanks to the services of Granite Registry, capital requirements for these banks were easily provided by First Bank attesting that they had adequate funds on deposit (even if they didn't) and the necessary due diligence was also performed by the same company controlled by Larry Barnabe and Van Brink without having to bother The Registrar, Michael Creft, with such minor details. As a result, eventually there were 18 sub-banks or trusts registered in Grenada and Nauru, all under the aegis of Van Brink's First Bank, none of them properly capitalised or managed. Their sole function was to bring in more funds through the Independent Contractors, commissioned agents who were already investors of some sort and had been sold IBC's to receive their commissions without having to trouble the taxman.

A typical example was Meridian Investment Bank whose board of directors included a former Florida plumber and two bankrupts, one of them still undischarged at the time of his appointment, a circumstance that should have automatically excluded him from office.

Wellington Bank and Trust was another, headed by John Brinker and Gary Bentz of Ohio, neither of whom had any banking background or experience.

Brinker and his wife had, however, much experience of lawsuits, having been on the receiving end of a good many over the years and having filed for bankruptcy in 1992. Then their assets were listed as $97,445 with liabilities of $463,316. Grenada's Offshore Banking Act required all directors of a bank licensed under the Act to have a net wealth in excess of two million dollars so it would seem that the bankruptcy had led to a rapid improvement in their financial affairs.

The income generated by these sub-banks for First Bank depended very largely on the creativity and salesmanship of their owners. One that achieved a considerable degree of success was Crown Meridian Bank, fronted by an old Maui acquaintance, Danny Hashimoto, who travelled on a Rhodesian passport, a country that no longer existed. His other claim to fame was that he had once beaten the IRS, but only by default as it later turned out. Another successful bank was Cambridge International Trust, run by David Rowe. Successful, in this context, meant the attracting of deposits, not their subsequent management, all the funds collected being deposited with First Bank or one of their many accounts with other banks.

In May 1999, a Danole Dykend, whose integrity may be judged from his use of at least three other assumed names, Dan Barr, Dan Van Dyke and Dan Dykend, aspired to the same lofty ideals and, as part of his deal, purchased a CD from First Bank in the sum of $300,205.23 that was payable, plus interest, on the 16th. of the following month. Why this was for a single month has never been explained as First Bank did not list any monthly CD's in their published literature but it can be assumed that this was a part of the arrangement between Brink and Dykend. Dykend then assigned this CD to his bank, Union Caribbean Bank Ltd., registered in Grenada and presumably set up by First Bank on his behalf (Van Brink later denied this and said that Dykend was only a "troublesome depositor"). On the appointed day, Dykend, accompanied by a Panos Maxos, his nominal manager of Union Caribbean, Anselm Clouden and Celia Edwards, attorneys for the bank, arrived in Young Street at First Bank's premises to attempt to cash the CD. From the number of attendees it seems apparent that Dykend suspected that his CD was not encashable, perhaps tipped off by Clouden who had previously been involved with First Bank. It is not usually necessary to have one's bank manager plus two attorneys in attendance for a simple transaction of this nature.

As he seems to have suspected, the receptionist at First Bank, Janice Duncan was unable to locate the bank's Comptroller, a Ms. Pauline Radix. A second receptionist, who wisely refused to give her name, said Ms. Radix was "around somewhere but was busy and unavailable". The CD was presented for payment but, unsurprisingly, was not honoured.

The party then trudged a few blocks to the office of The Registrar, Michael Creft, to register a formal complaint. He made a call and said that a representative from the bank would now be available to see them at 11:15 that day. Returning to the bank on time, they found that Ms. Radix was still unavailable but had left a letter for them explaining that the bank was not in a position to redeem the CD at such short notice. Frustrated, they left the building and subsequently filed a claim with the Supreme Court in Grenada for Breach of Contract, the first claim to be made against the bank to date. The claim remains outstanding to this day and the true story as much of a mystery as ever.

Unsettling though it must have been to Van Brink to have a depositor on the doorstep demanding restitution, it was probably the least of his concerns that June. His bête noir, David Marchant, had somehow unearthed the goods on his newly appointed auditor and was spreading the word via Offshore Alert that First Bank was now being audited by a de-frocked CPA, hardly a confidence inspiring bit of news. Furthermore, the FBI were now taking an interest in goings on at First Bank and enquiring of the government as to the situation. Loyally, Prime Minister Mitchell, mindful of his backers, assured them that everything was on the up and up with First Bank and with banking in Grenada in general.

Van Brink was also having to contend with the sometimes aberrant behaviour of the less than professional conmen who now acted as managers of his correspondent banks. In June, Rowe, CEO and President of Cambridge International Trust had been introduced by Sonia Novick, a commissioned representative, to Deo Singh, a wealthy prospective investor. At a meeting, Rowe, going one better than even the inflated promises of First Bank, offered an unbelievable 100% interest for six months for a deposit of $500,000 or more and stated that he would provide insurance valued at two to four times the value of the principal and interest of the Certificate of Deposit issued by Cambridge. Not content with using the handy, if mythical, facilities provided by IDIC for this insurance, Rowe came up with a story that Cambridge invested with Lines Overseas Management in Bermuda, who in turn were insured by Lloyds of London for up to $10 million per transaction. Ergo, Singh's investment was also insured by Lloyds of London, an even better insurance than IDIC. At a meeting in the San Francisco Marriott Hotel, Singh was introduced to Gerard Burns, allegedly Executive Vice President and Money Manager for Cambridge International Trust who provided a letter from their attorney, Waylon McMullen, attesting to this.

On or about June 21, 1999, McMullen, acting on behalf of CIT, sent the letter on his law office letterhead in which he advised Singh as follows:

> "You are advised that I have reviewed the documents regarding accounts opened at Lines Overseas Management Limited (LOM) as requested by Mr. David Rowe. All Lines Overseas Management Limited companies are regulated by the Monetary Authorities in their particular jurisdiction and employ full-time compliance departments. LOM carries significant insurance through Lloyds of London and insures each account up to ten million dollars ($10,000,000.00).
>
> Accordingly, I recommended you open separate accounts as needed to meet each individual need. Should you desire additional information, please give me a call."

There is no evidence of Cambridge having invested a single dollar with Lines Overseas Management and McMullen's letter neatly avoided the issue.

Singh's investment was to be by way of Intel shares in lieu of cash and he was told that the funds were to be used as collateral to buy a bank in Switzerland, named the Royal Bank of Zurich. The likelihood of being able to buy a Swiss bank with $500,000 does not seem to have occurred to him. The shares were to be returned to him plus interest within six months, on January 5th. 2000. Ursula Williams, Authorised Fiduciary Officer for Cambridge International Trust, signed the document.

Offshore scams depend for their success largely on the fact that the scammed usually have a strong objection to going to the authorities to report the matter. Sometimes this is due to sheer embarrassment at having fallen for the lies but usually it is due to the fact that they themselves, by investing offshore and concealing the fact, are in breach of their country's rules and regulations. In the United States in particular, the penalties can be severe, enough incentive to prevent the exposure of the scam. In Mr. Singh's case, the inexperienced Rowe had made an egregious error. Since his "investment" was by way of stock and moreover stock that was legally transferred and recorded by Charles Schwab in San Francisco to Pacific International Securities and Union Securities in Canada, there was nothing improper in his side of the deal. When his shares were not returned, Singh went to the FBI.

However, this was in the future although Van Brink felt the shadows lengthening daily on his sojourn in Grenada. But he was not yet finished and was by now investigating the possibilities available in Central Africa where he may have felt that his chequered career to date might not be a limiting factor. He claims to have been invited to go to Uganda but it seems likely that his trip was more opportunistic, an attempt to buy into a struggling bank in Kampala. Feeling the need for a little publicity boost for First Bank, now coming under a barrage of criticism from Marchant and others, at the end of July he arranged, although still rattling around in Uganda, for another inspiring press release, once again through the medium of WISE:

July 26, 1999

Breaking News from W.I.S.E.

First International Bank of Grenada (First Bank) is the guarantor of the mechanism (Stock Value Bank Guarantees) that promises investors of stocks purchased on WISE will never lose their investment. We feel it is important to keep you abreast of the unwarranted attacks on the integrity of First Bank and the results of the investigation that resulted from these unsubstantiated allegations. Therefore, we are printing a press release dated today.

Press Release, July 26, 1999
First Bank Says "Thanks!"

First International Bank of Grenada ("First Bank") today expressed its thanks to Prime Minister Dr. Keith Mitchell for having had the fortitude to resist the pressures of nay-sayers and objectively determine the facts concerning its banking operations.

"I feel completely vindicated in our decision to come to Grenada," said First Bank's Chairman Van A. Brink in a telephone interview from Uganda (Africa). Brink said that when the bank's organizers were considering the choice of a jurisdiction as the home of their offshore banking operations, they tried to evaluate which of many jurisdictions they felt would have the resilience to stand up to outside pressures, to abide by their own laws, and to carefully determine the facts before rushing to a decision.

"Offshore banking is not a popular thing among the governments of industrialized and heavily taxed nations", Brink said. "We knew that if we were successful, there would come a lot of pressure against us by way of unsubstantiated allegations and rumors. But even knowing this, we were shocked at the intensity of the attacks we received," Brink added.

Since early this year First Bank has been the target of allegations from many sources, including suggestions from seemingly credible persons that it might be engaged in money-laundering activities, one of the most damaging allegations that can be made against a financial institution. On Friday Prime Minister Mitchell gave a final report on the FBI investigation he had requested be conducted concerning First Bank and its officers and directors, noting that the FBI had concluded that there was no evidence of money-laundering or other criminal activities on the part of First Bank.

"*No one likes to sit still for a long investigative process,*" *said Brink,* "*but we were comforted by the even-handedness of the Prime Minister in refusing to give in to pressures in the absence of a thorough investigation and determination of the facts. We knew what the facts were, so we were confident of the final outcome, even though it is anything but pleasant to hold a 'stiff upper lip' in the face of constant criticism.*"

Brink noted that in the face of the outside adverse publicity, those who wanted to take advantage of the bank always prefaced their moves with threats of more bad publicity, if the bank wouldn't give them whatever it was they were asking.

"*It is nothing short of breath-taking how some people will try to exploit someone's unfortunate situation for their personal gain,*" *Brink said.* "*We decided early on that we would continue to do proper banking and business practice, no matter how much adverse publicity was generated by those who simply wanted to make spoil of the bank.*"

First Bank's Chairman also noted that the bank's commitment to its clients and to its community has remained resolute. "*We know who we are. We know what we're doing. And we know where we're going,*" *Brink said, noting that First Bank continues to pay its foreign depositors an aggressive rate of return, that it continues to offer all of its employees (from the least to the greatest) a wage scale on the leading-edge in Grenada, that its community and charitable giving worldwide has exceeded EC $1.3 million in the past six months, and that the bank intends to continue to try to* "*make a difference in the world.*"

Among projects that the bank recently has become involved with are those of establishing a hospital (Germany), a children's medical clinic (Uganda), a program for the education and care of "street kids"(Uganda), and other humanitarian and development projects (liberated territory of the Democratic Republic of Congo).

"*There is so much to do, not just at home in Grenada, but all around the world,*" *Brink said.* "*It is time for those in the financial services industry to look at more than the bottom line profit and to put their creative juices to work on how to solve some of the problems all around us,*" *he commented.*

Brink concluded by saying, "*Now that any reasonable basis for the negative press has been put to rest in our home jurisdiction, we are hopeful that First Bank's involvement in the Grenadian community will be welcomed as well.*"

As with so many of Van Brink's humanitarian projects, no evidence of any of these mentioned has ever surfaced during subsequent investigations and it is unlikely that Prime Minister Mitchell welcomed the unwanted publicity surrounding him and First Bank that the announcement generated.

It seemed that the time was now appropriate for readying the lifeboat and the compliant Michael Creft was once again induced to pen a letter, this time to the authorities in Uganda. Addressed to The Chairman, Committee National Economy at The Parliament, Kampala, Uganda, the letter read:

Re: First International Bank of Grenada.

Under Grenada's system of government, the Minister of Finance has regulatory oversight in all areas of the offshore industry, which is done through this office.

First International Bank of Grenada Limited is registered in Grenada and according to our records is in good standing. It has grown to be Grenada's leading offshore bank.

According to audited financial statements submitted by the bank, it is in a healthy financial position.

Should you have any specific questions, the office will endeavour to respond in any way possible as you conduct your due diligence.

Yours truly,

Michael Creft,
Registrar, Offshore Financial Services.

As the bank had so far failed to provide any audited accounts, Creft's reference to them could only have been a figment of his, or perhaps Van Brink's, imagination.

Meanwhile the seminars, arranged by The Offshore Educational Institute, continued to reel in the unwary to be seduced by the poolside at the Rex Grenadian. It is a tribute to the salesmanship of the Van Brink team that so few attendees failed to question just how a relatively new bank could distribute such largesse when other more venerable institutions could not, but much depended on the testimony of the IC's who were receiving their interest payments on time along with their commissions in the manner perfected by Mr. Ponzi.

But the drumbeat of retribution was becoming ever louder during that summer as more and more journalists and government bodies started casting their eyes over First Bank and the ever expanding hydra of associates.

14

The Bank of World Peace

Never far from the background in all of First Bank's dealings were the quasi-religious overtones and pseudo philosphical mutterings of the protagonists.

A typical example was the "Mission Statement" from Wellington Bank and Trust:

> *"At Wellington Bank and Trust, we believe first and foremost that we are but stewards of those things which God has entrusted to our care.*
>
> *It is with this realisation always in mind that we continually endeavour to conduct the affairs of Wellington Bank and Trust with the highest level of integrity and character.*
>
> *We absolutely believe that there is a very real Heaven to gain and an equally as real Hell to shun. We also absolutely believe the Lord will return some day and that we cannot behave as though we have infinite time.*
>
> *We will constantly be working to take the "coin of the realm" (money is the coin of this world) in order to convert it into the "coin of the True Kingdom" (in layman's terms, to support the preaching of the Gospel).*
>
> *Because of our belief, Wellington Bank and Trust will always be pledging a sizeable percentage of its gross profit toward that end.*
>
> *In addition, we will seek to assist those who labour for the Lord by providing business ventures and cooperative agreements with those who are also like-minded."*

Not totally prepared to put all their trust in God, the bank prudently asked clients "to declare under penalty of perjury that I am not involved in any Government "sting" operation," a request that should have triggered alarm bells in any reasonable person's mind.

Less religiously but more earthily inclined, The Saatva Bank of World Peace was a good and successful example of how to play on the heartstrings of the gullible in order to separate them from their wallets. Managed by one, Tansen Sumeru, a slender, balding, middle-aged white American who wore silky pajamas and robes, with his hair flowing down his back and mustaches that reached down to his chest, he was accompanied by his "spiritual," but presumably also earthly, consort, Shirsha. Sumeru was a speaker at many of the Offshore Educational Institutes seminars, where he promoted his book *Sovereignty Consciousness,* available for a mere $17 on line he would point out, along with his theory that new technology is making the traditional concept of government outdated. His message was that every person could be a world citizen—in effect, his or her own sovereign, with no allegiance or obligations, including the requirement to pay taxes to governments formed under the old notion of nationhood. Like Van Brink, he had changed his name "for spiritual reasons" from a rather more worldly David Freeston (he had also used several other names in the past) and had previously been peddling a dubious offshore investment programme called Quantum Gold based in The Bahamas. When that had failed to produce results and the investors were proving cantankerous, he attempted to divert his frustrated clients to his new bank.

Publicity for the bank's principals described them as; "Wayshowers in a rapidly growing international network of highly conscious people evolving new paradigms of world peace and enlightened capitalism," a statement that should have confused any student of the English language.

One investor in his project said the thing that attracted him to Sattva Bank was Sumeru's assurance that the bank's emphasis was going to be on attracting investors who wanted to use their high returns for good works. "It was philanthropic. It was a way to make money and to do good," said the investor, who had done considerable volunteer work with charities and foundations. "One person wanted to start a cancer clinic, and they thought the bank would help." Other investors were raising money for foundations and charitable programs to help children, the poor and deprived ethnic minorities, he said. "A lot of people today are trying to reconcile spirituality and money. Here's a guy who comes along and says he's figured that out. They take your vision or your project you're involved with, and they describe how you can accomplish that. It's a pretty compelling thing," he said. The investor added that he had hoped to make enough money to finance a new charitable foundation of his own. He admitted, however, that 200% annual returns also were attractive to him as a personal investor, and so was Sumeru's offer for each investor to become a "conduit" or agent who could get commissions for getting their friends and relatives to make deposits, too.

"The bank attracted a certain kind of people—naïve, for sure, but they were interested in putting forward some kind of social project," the California investor said. "They played upon the good intentions of the investors. It was so insidious." He said that when he complained to Sumeru and other officials of Sattva Bank, they claimed that they had lost their money, too, by being involved with First Bank and warned him that asking questions could jeopardize the return of everybody's money. "That enabled them to say they were in the same boat we were in. There was a lot of blaming the victims. They said, 'Because you're asking questions, you're creating fear.' Their response was, 'That hurts what we're trying to do.' He concluded: "I can't tell you how many people I've heard from who have been devastated, common people—people from all over the world, people living on farms, people trying to send their kids to college."

The Sattva Investment Bank, the Bank of World Peace, would pay interest of up to 200% a year on certificates of deposit, Sumeru said. Many Quantum Gold investors also put money into Sattva as Sumeru explained that Sattva Bank would earn its remarkable returns not from uncertain commodities trading, like Quantum Gold where returns had proved elusive, but from "high-yield investment programs" operating in complex, little-known areas of high finance typically available only to the top banks in the world. According to Sumeru and others who promote them through small offshore banks, these prime bank instruments, also known as "prime bank debentures," "prime bank guarantees," "medium term notes," and "standby letters of credit," allowed the World Bank, the Federal Reserve and the biggest banks in the world to move money back and forth by discounting large notes they traded among themselves. A key selling point used by Sumeru and the many others who promote prime bank instruments around the world is that governments and large banks do not want investors to know that such notes even exist. He told his investors: "Banks will tell you these notes don't exist. Government agencies will tell you that you're being swindled. Don't listen to them. They're just trying to keep these huge profits for themselves." The sales pitch appealed to the many people who were suspicious of governments and banks anyway and who thought that "the establishment" was conspiring to hoard wealth and keep common people from getting rich, too. Sumeru warned them that no one would confirm the existence of prime bank notes and, sure enough, no one did.

Taansen Sumeru's Sattva Bank was supposed to have access to these high-yield bank trading programs through The First International Bank of Grenada, just another head of the Hydra.

15

Looking to the East

Rather as he had viewed Grenada only a short while previously, Van Brink was now looking to the African continent as his new playground. He had already attempted to establish himself there by making a bid to take over the ailing Co-op Bank in Kampala but had been brusquely rebuffed. As a local paper there reported it:

> *The Bank of Uganda rejected a bankrupt 'briefcase' investor brought in by the defunct Cooperative Bank board, the Bank Probe Commission heard yesterday.*
>
> *Outgoing Governor Nyonyintono Kikonyogo told the commission that the central bank was trying to avoid a repeat of the Westmont saga (a previous banking disaster). He said the investor claimed he was from the First International Bank of Grenada.*
>
> *Kikonyogo said the man, Van Brink, said he wanted to invest US$5m (over sh5b) into the Cooperative Bank, but investigations showed that he was not credible.*
>
> *The Cooperative Bank had a net insolvency of sh5.4b at the time it was seized.*
>
> *Kikonyogo said it was found the investor lacked experience in commercial banking and that he had been declared bankrupt in other countries.*
>
> *"We discovered that he had no banking experience anywhere and had been declared bankrupt in a few countries...now that is not the kind of person we would want to invite here. Besides, we had experienced problems of Westmont here...," Kikonyogo said.*

Although he must have been surprised at the speed at which bad news had reached Kampala, he pressed on with his plans to launch the lifeboat in that direction. He had extended his stay in Uganda and had met with Prince Willy of the Democratic Republic of Congo. Incredibly, he proposed to Prince Willy, who clearly was not a subscriber to Offshore Alert, that he could help set up a financial structure for his nation. In his own words written much later:

"I finally told Prince Willy that he'd have to start from the ground up with a monetary system backed with substance that the world could not help by recognize and a general economic development program designed for the benefit of his people. He said something to the essence of, "Yes, that's what I want; that's what my people need. Can you write it out? If you'll write it, I'll make sure it is presented to all of the factions now fighting in the country—I know most of the leaders personally. You write it; I'll make sure it gets read by the right people."

My passion as a young man was the study of economics and economic philosophy. Not many students of economics are ever called upon to suggest an economic and monetary system to a struggling nation. I told Prince Willy to give me a few days to outline what I thought might work and I'd get back to him with a draft proposal.

I was then consumed with the rethinking and integrating of several concepts I had been working on through the years. I extended my stay in Kampala and mixed meetings with shareholder representatives of the failed bank (and drafting a proposal they found acceptable) with spending the rest of my waking hours formulating the basics of a document I now simply refer to as "The Plan."

"The Plan" does not call for giving me gold or diamonds, but for using such internationally respected items as the backing for a new currency. The DRC happens to have some of the most significant gold and diamond fields (and other precious and strategic minerals) in the world, yet it languishes in abject national poverty. What is wrong with this picture?

I have often been accused in the press of funding one or more rebel movements in the DRC. I have not contributed (or caused to be contributed) one dollar to aid in the process of Congolese killing their fellow Congolese. Instead, I offered to help negotiate humanitarian aid packages proposed by any and all belligerents in the turmoil, as well as by civil (non military) groups. I hoped that if the peace could be made attractive enough, it would be embraced and the Congolese could get on with healing themselves and their nation together."

Quite what Prince Willy made of "The Plan" when he got it is unknown. Undoubtedly Brink had put a lot of effort into the work in terms of the sheer physical length of the document but, as with much of his windy writings, there tended to be more hype than substance and the economic proposals made were nebulous and impracticable, most notably in the absence of any clue as to how the project was to have been funded, all the participants being impoverished nations. He did, however, go at length into areas usually neglected by economists, the design of the bank notes for the consortium, for instance.

"Design of the New Currency: On the obverse of the note, utilize multi-national, happy children playing. On the reverse side, utilize pictures of African animals. Such a theme could be carried out for both coins and paper currency (the currency should be printed by four color process). Since we are instituting one of the most

valuable currencies in the world, let us also make it the most attractive currency in the world.

Possible motto: "Our future depends on all of us"

Universally, children are seen as being the future of a family and of a nation. All parents wish to see a bright future for their children.

Instituting an asset-backed currency establishes a sound financial base upon which the future may be developed.

On paper currency, signatures by a participating nation's Minister of Finance and by the AURS Comptroller of the Currency. A color flag of the nation next to the Minister's signature. Seals screened in background for both the participating nation and the AURS. French language with English sub-titles. Sizing: English Pound note sizes, since increasing note denomination sizes allow for increasingly legible sub-titles, as well as for the ease of sorting the currency."

And then there was his innovative scheme for disposing of the old, displaced currency.

"Use by the Reserve of the old currency: The old currency will not be destroyed, but will be warehoused until the expiration of exchange value.

The notes will then be bundled for sale as "game money" and "poker money" to consumers worldwide. "One Hundred Thousand Francs" ($29.95) or "Be a Millionaire" (only $149.95) or "Genuine Counterfeit Francs" (only $49.95).

In the packages of game money, the AURS would insert a color brochure describing the new currency, its backing, a pictorial tour of the participating nation, the wild animals in their natural habitat, a brief history of the country, an invitation for tourism ("We'll greet you with free money samples, if you come." and "[Name of Nation]—Absolutely priceless, and worth every carat.")

The object, here, is not to make a fortune selling canceled or counterfeit currency (although the additional foreign currency proceeds could prove useful), but to expose the world to the new asset-backed currency of the participating nation. For the country to emerge as a world financial center services nation, the world must become intimately introduced to what it is that the nation has to offer.

It could be that demand for the "game money" old currency will out pace the supply of the redeemed old currency. The makers of the board game called Monopoly, for instance, print more face value in game money each day than does the Federal Reserve System. For this reason, the plates for printing the old currency should be retained in the physical possession of the Reserve (and the Reserve will ultimately need to construct its own bank-note production facility for absolute control of both the genuine new currency and the genuine old currency)."

Also included in the scheme was a mention of that old standby of FIBG, The World Investors Stock Exchange, with its guaranteed investments.

An Ancillary Component Strategy—The World Investors' Stock Exchange:
  Both onshore and offshore corporations may list their stocks for public trading.
  Unlike other stock exchanges, the capital of investors is guaranteed through Stock
  Value Guarantees issued by the Reserve.

The total impossibility of being able to "guarantee" investor's funds in any publicly traded stock is an indication of the outlandish fiscal thinking of Brink despite his claims to a degree in economics and a life-long interest in the subject. The document remains an interestingly idealised concept, however flawed, and it seems a pity that the author's obvious talents could not have been put to better use. There is a complete version in Appendix C.

Meanwhile, back in Grenada, some local entertainment was now provided by Van Brink flying in, at the bank's expense, a group of officials from his new chums in the Congo. While travelling in the Congo, in addition to Prince Willy, he had met Ernest Wamba dia Wamba, leader of one of the Congolese rebel groups trying to overthrow the government of Laurent Kabila. In 1999 they announced a deal. In the event that Wamba came to power, Brink would have the right to set up a central bank and a new monetary system for the Congo. There was also a deal concerning the mineral rights underlying the nation in which Brink showed a special interest. In exchange, Brink would provide the Congo with $16 million, which was to be spent upgrading the troubled country's roads and hospitals.

Wamba, a former Harvard lecturer, initially dismissed reports of Van Brinks problems with First Bank saying "Any time you have a fundamental change in the world economy, in this case a shift from classical banks to offshore banks, there are sure to be clashes." He very soon changed his opinion.

In one of the flamboyant moves that were his trademark, Brink flew a delegation of fifty of Wamba's supporters to Grenada for a celebration of the partnership. Taxi drivers in Grenada, who benefited greatly from the sudden influx of affluent dignitaries, still remember wistfully this unexpected bonanza. But the honeymoon barely lasted beyond the first round of cocktails at the poolside bar. As had the Ugandans earlier, the rebel Congolese contingent soon got wind of Brink's less than sparkling financial record, settled for few days enjoying themselves at the bank's expense, and then tore up the agreement.

Later a Kampala newspaper reported the affair. According to New Vision, Brink signed an agreement in June 1999 with the Rally for Congolese Democracy, a Congolese rebel group led by Ernest Wamba dia Wamba and several tribal chiefs in eastern part of the Congo, to set up an entity called the African Union

Reserve System. The African Union Reserve System was to run mining projects and Congo's central bank for 60 years in return for a 35% commission paid to the Congolese government when Wamba took power.

Under the deal to come into effect if the rebels captured state power, Brink was expected to advance US$1 billion to re-boot the economy. A special security force of Congolese trained by foreigners would be set up to protect the bank. 'But the rebels now say the US$48 million deal was a hoax,' the newspaper stated. 'They said Brink used the agreement to hoodwink other banks for funds.'

Allegedly Brink used the paperwork from the contract to obtain loans for his own use. 'We were conned,' a Congolese tribal chief was quoted as stating. 'We saw him (Brink) as a saviour to our numerous problems, but we are now disappointed because we have never seen this man produce or do anything he pledged.' In an interview with the newspaper, Brink told them that the Congo operation could no longer work because of lack of funding from the FIBG. He said he had set up African Union Reserve System as an implementing partner for the funds to be released by the Grenada bank, but some 'powerful forces' had sabotaged the system.

It was now apparent from the noise in the marketplace that the name of Van Brink was no longer much of a cachet for any financial institution, even in the Congo, and urgent remedial action was called for to restore some of the sheen to First Bank. The board of directors convened the members, preceded by a prayer meeting to guide them in their decisions, a process that seems to have been a standard practice at First Bank.

Whether the answer came through prayer or commonsense will never be known but in the end it was decided that Van Brink should step down as CEO and Chairman in the best interests of the bank. An advertisement in the Grenada Today newspaper ran:

> "The Board of Directors of First International Bank of Grenada Limited wishes to advise the General and Investing Public that Mr. Van Brink, formerly known as Gilbert Ziegler, is no longer associated with First International Bank of Grenada Limited either directly or indirectly. Further, Mr. Van Brink is NOT Authorised to conduct any business on behalf of or in the name of First International Bank of Grenada."

Stirring stuff and, in keeping with most of the bank's statements, totally false. Van Brink was still as much in charge as ever.

Perhaps feeling that this brusque announcement did not paint him in a very favourable light, some months later, Brink posted a more comfortable and flattering explanation on the Internet:

> *"When I finally returned to Grenada from Kampala, I resigned as Chairman of the Board/CEO of First Bank (October 1, 1999) so that I could devote full time to trying to do what I could to help the Congolese and the African peoples via the Union Reserve System and African Union Reserve System."*

Van Brink's successor was to be Mark Kennedy, the former antenna expert from WISE, who had been Chief Operating Officer of the bank for several months. The appointment, like the assets of the bank and the press statement, was purely a fiction. Van Brink remained at the helm.

What was not fictional was the dire necessity of finding an auditor for the bank following the revelations concerning Craig and his associate, who, it was now revealed, had also been convicted of bank fraud previously. They came up with a Barry Mathews, CPA, who sent a letter of acceptance to Mark Kennedy on the 9th. of October and who then set to work to unravel the convoluted accounts at the bank.

Meanwhile there was another letter from Creft to the bank itself in October 1999, stating that the FBI in the United States had cleared of it wrongdoing following an investigation. Creft wrote:

> *"Earlier this year it came to the attention of the Offshore Financial Services Division that serious allegations were being made against The First International Bank of Grenada. The allegations concerned money laundering and other illicit activities.*
>
> *The Government of Grenada took the allegations seriously and sought the assistance of the Federal Bureau of Investigation. The FBI carried out an investigation into the activities, procedures and associations of First Bank. They also made enquiries and checks with respect to the source of many deposits.*
>
> *I can confirm that the results of the investigation has exonerated First Bank regarding the allegations. The procedures adopted by First Bank with respect to all deposits are more than adequate to ensure that all deposits received into the bank are clean funds and from legitimate sources."*

The accuracy of Creft's claim, however, was questionable since, only a month later, U.S. Assistant Attorney Claire Fay wrote to Grenada's government:

> *"As you are aware,"* she said, *"the Federal Bureau of Investigation is involved in an ongoing investigation of the First International Bank of Grenada, bank president Gilbert A. Ziegler [Van Brink]…and various associates of the bank and Mr. Ziegler. The FBI has evidence indicating that Mr. Ziegler, his associates, and FIBG are engaging in conduct constituting fraud and money laundering."*

The letter, dated November 12, 1999, and made public in connection with a lawsuit filed against First Bank, then made a series of remarkable allegations. Fay wrote that the FBI had tracked down the real owner of First Bank's famous ruby, who said he had owned the gem for twenty years and during that time had never sold or leased it to anyone. Moreover, he had never heard of First Bank, Resource Enhancement or Van Brink either. Fay also warned that a $50-million bank guarantee issued by the First Bank, signed by Brink and provided to the Grenadian offshore officials was also probably bogus. She expressed equal scepticism about First Bank's arrangement with the International Depositor Insurance Corporation, which had been turfed off the Caribbean island of Nevis after it was found to be operating without a licence. Included in the letter was an offer from the FBI to assist in a raid on First Bank's premises.

Once again, the government did nothing.

The raid never took place, the government ignored the offer and FIBG was allowed to continue in the business of robbing more innocent citizens of their hard earned money.

Planning ahead, Van Brink had by this time arranged to wire $1.3 million to an account in Kampala to be used for accomodation for himself when the time came. It was eventually used to purchase a house just outside Kampala. Later the investment by the bank in Uganda climbed to $3.7 million and then even higher.

Kampala was looking more and more attractive.

16

Running on Empty

Van Brink's resignation did little to quiet the rumors now flooding the media about First Bank and, as the year drew to a close, there was a significant decrease in the inflow of funds. Since the bank, as it was later proved, had made no investments with depositor's funds to generate any income, the only revenue to pay off clients had to come from new deposits and they were rapidly running dry.

The year turned and with it the fortunes of First Bank. On the 6th.of January, the new auditor, Mathews, issued a "compilation report" on the accounts at First Bank but declined to provide an audit or even a review, having met with the same stumbling blocks that had prevented Wilson and Co. from completing the work. Grenada had re-vamped, to some extent, its offshore surveillance and had formed GIFSA, Grenada International Financial Services Authority, a committee that would, it was hoped, put some muscle (but not too much) into the policing of banks and trust companies. It did, however, still include Michael Creft as chairman, who by now had been christened "the village idiot of regulators" by David Marchant, still in hot pursuit of his quarry.

Mark Kennedy, who, for all the kudos of his appointment, seems to have been left in the dark as to the real position of First Bank, soldiered on as best he could. Clients were already having problems withdrawing from their accounts using the debit cards provided. These came from an entity registered in St. Vincent and The Grenadines but were processed via a bank in Costa Rica.

Conveniently, First Bank had total control and authority over these. The excuse given for their not being honoured was that there was a language problem at the bank and that, as a result, accounts were not being properly credited. They claimed First Bank's Spanish speaking representative in St. Vincent had left the company causing a hiatus in communication. As any visitor to Central America can confirm, the standard of English spoken and written in the business world there is remarkably high and hardly likely to have caused any errors. But it was a convenient excuse.

By now Van Brink must have felt that the hounds were snapping at his heels a little too closely for comfort and at the end of the month he quietly left Grenada and his floundering bank. Travelling by way of Havana, Cuba, to avoid having to transit the United States, where he felt they might be interested in interviewing him, he arrived in Kampala, via London. His companion on the trip was a woman named Jagoda whose presence was never satisfactorily explained but whose boy friend had been financed by FIBG to go into business. She did prove her worth in Cuba however when Van Brink's credit card was declined, proving there was some justice in the world after all, and they were only able to proceed by using her personal debit card.

They landed in Entebbe, Uganda on the 4th.of February, Van Brink's birthday. What happened to the mysterious Jagoda and why she went to Uganda is unknown but Van Brink moved into the house on the Mbuya Hill complex, Kampala for which the investors with the bank had unwittingly paid $1.3 million. Undoubtedly his presence in Uganda was not particularly welcome in view of the frosty reception he had received the previous year with his attempted takeover of the Cooperative Bank, now owned by Standard Chartered. The government wished to know just what Van Brink was going to bring to Uganda as a condition of his being allowed to stay.

He wrote a lengthy E-Mail to his old friend Tai, who wisely appears to have left Grenada for the US by this time, with a copy to the beleaguered Mark Kennedy, stipulating his severance terms from the bank. In view of his knowledge of the true position it is a remarkable document in which he asks for a retainer of $30,000 per month as consultancy fees adjusted to 10% of bank earnings to be paid to his IBC, Workingdraft Publications Ltd., at an unrelated financial institution. Workingdraft Publications was to have been the publisher for a book he claimed to be working on entitled New Millenium Economics, an ambitious title for a man who had, to date, only demonstrated a talent for salesmanship and embezzlement.

The E-Mail was an extraordinarily revealing document listing as it did the properties purchased by the bank in Uganda (properties that he later denied having any association with) plus many other transactions. The tone of the message implies that all is still well and that the bank is a functioning and profitable operation not the collapsing pyramid that he knew it to be. It is as if he has become so accustomed to deluding investors that he has himself become a victim of his own lies.

He mentions that, in order for him to remain in Uganda "with some amount of governmental protection and security", an ominous requirement, he must meet accredited investor standards with the government who appear to have been pressing him on the point. Details of the disposal of some company cars follow, winding up with a request for a blue bracelet and "that we'll always be friends."

A final tear-jerking paragraph protests that he always tried to do his best and that he still would, ending, "Love, Van."

Clearly the flight from Grenada was precipitate as he appears to have left a good deal of material and effects behind that one would have thought he would have needed in his new location. Among these were the hard drives off his computers, the contents of which were later obtained mysteriously by a gleeful David Marchant, who reported in his Offshore Alert that most of the bookmarks pointed to porn sites. Some months later, Van Brink posted a wordy response on a public bulletin board to explain:

> *David Marchant (Offshore Alert) has just published that my computer hard drive in Grenada was analyzed and revealed that I viewed porn sites on the web whenever I wasn't busy stealing depositors' money.*
>
> *I comment to openly acknowledge the lengths Mr. Marchant's sources will go to accomplish their agenda.*
>
> *In fact there were some porn sites bookmarked on my computer browser in Grenada. It happened that I had a young man come in and hook me up for Internet communications (theretofore I had only used word processing and a fax program—that there was probably 100,000+such files of correspondence items and contract documents on my computer or reduced to a dozen zip disks isn't mentioned). I left the young man here for a couple hours while I went to a lunch meeting.*
>
> *When I returned the young man lectured me, observing that I didn't have any games on my computer (he showed me where he had loaded a couple dozen of his favorites). And since I lived alone, he figured all work and no play was not a good recipe for happy single male life and he demonstrated to me how to access the bookmarked porn sites he had created for my enjoyment. I thanked him for his thoughtfulness. And when he left I went back to work.*
>
> *But who has had my hard disk and other files since August 11, 2000? The appointees of the Government of Grenada, PWC/Wide, and I believe probably the FBI.*
>
> *Watch "Enemy of the State" (a movie) sometime. There is a scene where the movie's bad guy wants to know everything he can about the movie's good guy so he can use it against him. He calls for his high-tech computer geeks to dig up everything they can find—what movies the man has rented, whether he views porn on the internet, if he's had any affairs—anything at all that he can use to discredit the movie's good guy in the public media.*
>
> *Let's call the movie "art."*

Now consider for just a moment in what ways you may now personally witness real life imitating art.

Or is it that the art actually WAS trying to tell those of us who would find it hard to believe, but highly entertaining, something about how real life is these days?

Van

P.S. Yes, I have actually viewed porn sites on the Internet. No, I didn't steal the money.

This fatuous rebuttal can only have greatly increased Marchant's enjoyment.

Back in Grenada, Mark Kennedy was having an increasingly difficult time. By now the inflow of funds was down to a mere trickle and that trickle was being supplied by the few independent contractors who had not as yet realised that the game was virtually up and that their chances of ever receiving their commissions, to say nothing of the return of their capital, were zero. As far as Kennedy was concerned, First Bank wasn't hurting from bad PR so much as a "liquidity problem." In a letter to depositors in April 2000, he blamed delays in interest payments on problems arising from First Bank's rapid growth. He promised that the situation would soon improve.

But even as Kennedy drafted the letter, the problem was much worse than he let on. By then the bank, which so recently had claimed to be the world's most profitable, was struggling to meet its own payroll. Now finding it difficult to pay his staff, interest payments to clients finally ceased and the complaints started to roll in. Sometimes these could be fobbed off with the story that they were the problems of the correspondent bank involved and that First Bank would resolve them—in time. Some were more serious. Mr. Singh had already gone to the FBI with his complaint concerning Cambridge Bank (it had received a full banking licence in October, courtesy of Granite Registry) and the wheels were in motion to apprehend David Rowe, the principal.

As the money ran out, so did the major players associated with First Bank. Kennedy lacked the charisma of Brink to keep the team together and, taking whatever loot they could with them, they drifted back to Canada and the United States, hoping to disappear into the mists before the final crunch came. Larry Barnabe headed for Las Vegas where he was soon joined by the Jeddelohs to found International Learning Center, forming tax-free corporations in Nevada. Bob Skirving was in the northwest, about to form a new bank of his own, Bank of the Nations, on much the same lines as First Bank but located in Nauru.

A small core of the still faithful (and possibly clueless) were left behind to cope with an increasingly difficult financial situation. This was not improved as Van Brink had called earlier and demanded that $400,000 be wired to his account in Kampala. Despite protests from Regale that this could have been used to pay off some of the increasingly vociferous creditors, Brink insisted.

First Bank needed an injection of capital urgently if it were to survive at all. Kennedy, who appears to have been singularly naïve, turned to the supposed assets of the bank and found, to nobody else's surprise, that if not downright fraudulent they were certainly downright uncashable. Brink then had Richard Downes fly to Grenada to sort matters out with Kennedy who now seemed to be less than helpful in his attitude. In fact he refused to turn many documents over to Downes until compelled to do so by Van Brink and his newly appointed fixer, British barrister Lawrence Jones QC.

Desperate, he turned back to his mentor in Uganda for advice. The advice appears not to have been encouraging (in fact Brink had advised the Board to get rid of him) for Kennedy packed his bags, scooped as much cash as possible from the crumbling enterprise and removed himself and his new family to The Bahamas and thence to Florida. Shortly after, The Chief Financial Officer for First Bank, Rita Regale, also abandoned the sinking ship and followed to Florida.

"Fools rush in where fools have been before."

—Anon.

17

The Downes Recovery Plan

If anything was to be retrieved from the disaster now looming ahead for First Bank, a top priority had to be the calming of the fears of the now highly nervous depositors.

Already one group had attempted to encash one of the CD's they held with predictable results and, as a result, were preparing to enforce a Mareva Injunction which they hoped would prevent any assets being removed from the jurisdiction, unaware that they had already disappeared.

The new Chairman and CEO, Richard Downes, then published a so-called "recovery plan" designed to prevent any further such boat-rocking activity. Despite its length and complexity it is worth quoting in full, not only for its breathtaking hypocrisy, but because it gives a valuable insight into the convoluted thinking now pervading the management of the bank. The full text can be found in Appendix A.

Referring to the bank's current problems as a "liquidity crisis", Downes reverts to the alleged $4.2 billion of gold deposited at UBS (Switzerland), now apparently held as a bearer certificate by an unnamed California securities corporation with the receipt in the name of First Bank, and proposes using this to negotiate with IDIC for the purpose of obtaining an audit, liquidating the asset and using the funds to pay off all claims against First Bank or its subsidiaries. Estimating a time scale of 4-6 weeks for this apparently simple solution, it rather begs the question of why nobody had thought of it before or even why IDIC, a.k.a. Douglas Ferguson, needed to be involved.

Apparently unsure of the success of this ploy, Downes goes on to say that First Bank were currently negotiating with a major world financial group (unidentified) for some $21 billion in funding which, once again, would put First Bank back on the gravy train. This was, apparently, only possible if First Bank remained in business, i.e. was not shut down by the government or by aggrieved depositors, who, it was hinted darkly, would be shooting themselves in the foot if they attempted such a foolish action. The likelihood of any "world financial group" stumping up $21 billion for a bankrupt shady bank did not enter into the equation it seemed.

The ace in the hole was, however, the project to sell Preferred Shares in First Bank, $120 million dollars worth against the Certificates of Deposit issued by the the Bank of China, to those already mired in First Bank's tentacles. It seemed that the lucky depositors could obtain 5 shares for every dollar they had already invested and that the key to success would then be the ability to accept fresh deposits. This was, of course, contingent on the bank staying open and everybody keeping quiet about their claims. To encourage this thought, Downes stated:

> *"First Bank has present access to other proven investment programs. No re-opening of the bank's doors to deposit inflows can occur if the bank remains under threat of a closure or a supervised liquidation action by the Government of Grenada."*

Needless to say, no details were forthcoming of the proven investment programmes and quite what the bank was proposing to use for funds to invest, in view of its liquidity crisis, was not explained. But the bank had even more options:

> *E. As relates to other income/liquidity producing efforts related to First Bank:*
>
> 1. *One of the bank's holding companies is finalizing a credit line negotiation with a major financial institution in which US $53 million in financial instruments will be used to secure a credit line following the scenario outlined in item IV, above.*
>
>   *The roll out would be approximately US $10 million monthly. Negotiations are presently set for finalization within two weeks.*
>
> 2. *The same holding company is in a separate negotiation with another bank concerning US $250 million in financial instruments and producing a net future return of approximately US $39.6 million monthly.*
>
> 3. *The same holding company is negotiating the re-sale of some of its financial instruments for immediate cash to put forward to First Bank.*
>
> 4. *The same holding company has nine other negotiations underway on various projects, each of which would produce a financial return to First Bank within 30-90 days.*

Possibly these were the negotiations supposedly being conducted by Bob Skirving with the assistance of Van Brink in London during July/August 2000. Skirving and Brink were still in London when the Government of Grenada seized FIBG on August 11, 2000. They claimed they had successfully negotiated the placement of US $855 million in insured assets that FIBG owned to establish a line of credit from which the bank would have gained sufficient liquidity to bring all depositor obligations current. The Government of Grenada's appointed administrator of FIBG, Mr. Garvey Louison, and his successor, Erroll Thomas, wisely declined to accept their word that such a deal really existed, knowing the true status of the bank's alleged assets and bearing in mind the principal's serious difficulties with the truth in the past.

The statement concludes with a selection of the various options available—strongly advocating that depositors vote to keep the bank open and toss more cash its way. Waxing eloquent on the subject of "the vision" as perceived by Van Brink, the document has some inspiring quotes from Nelson Mandela and urges the faithfull, if slightly currently disenchanted, to hang in there—the crock of gold is just around the corner, it's just that the rainbow has had a bit of a hiccup.

The more perceptive readers might have been tempted to question why an establishment that held such enormous assets and could command such huge loans from world financial institutions had ever had a liquidity problem in the first place.

Few bank depositors can have ever received such a load of claptrap from their manager and few managers can ever have had such a low esteem for their client's intelligence to imagine that any of them would believe such nonsense. Interestingly, the statement flatly contradicted previous claims that Van Brink was no longer at the controls, it seems he was still there, promoting his "vision," even if his physical self was in faroff Uganda, and it is difficult not to sense his penmanship at work.

Despite this impassioned *mea culpa*, which would not appear to have been the unaided composition of Downes, the Government of Grenada remained singularly unimpressed for once and prepared to take control of the bank.

"Liars when they speak the truth are not believed."

—**Aristotle (384 BC–322 BC)**

18

A Queen's Counsel at the Helm.

With Downes now ensconced as the nominal head of First Bank, Van Brink continued to pull the strings from far off Kampala. Depositors were urged that the delays in reimbursements were temporary and depositors were encouraged to keep on coming. Downes' recovery plan was floated before the bemused eyes of the investors who were invited to vote on it. Rumours were floated of a multi-billion dollar investment from Switzerland that was to be received at any moment but it was yet another of Van Brink's fantasies and nothing ever came of it.

Realising that he needed to put some muscle into the operation if he was to continue to benefit from it, Brink had engaged a British barrister, Lawrence Jones QC to fly to Grenada and support Downes with his expertise. His abilities had been proved earlier when he was able to block the attempts by the FBI to obtain a search and seizure warrant for First Bank's premises and Van Brink must have felt that here was the man to pull the chestnuts from the fire. He offered him $60,000 per month to do so. Not surprisingly, Lawrence, a member of a highly reputable law firm in London (they had 17 attorneys attached to the London Chambers of Geoffrey Vos Q. C., one of the leading barristers in London and were highly-respected), arrived in Grenada with alacrity, together with a friend and colleague, Barclay Butler to assist him. He would have seemed to have been well qualified for the post, specialising in chancery, commercial banking, partnership and bankruptcy law and being qualified to practice law in England & Wales from 1988, as well as in Australia and Grenada.

Having reviewed the documents of the bank he seemed as bemused as others had been before him and E-Mailed Van Brink saying that, "I must rely heavily on you to answer specific questions concerning the bank's asset base." He went on to request that Van Brink made himself available to himself, the Board and the auditors to provide documentary details of the asset base as he had left it and to try and clarify a "very confusing situation", as he called it with masterly understatement. He held meetings with Prime Minister Keith Mitchell, the Director of

Public Prosecutions, Hugh Wildman; a Grenada Supreme Court Judge, Justice Saint-Paul; and the President of the Grenada Bar Association, Attorney Reynold Benjamin.

In a letter to FIBG officer Rita Regale concerning his previous intervention on behalf of the bank Jones had written: "I do not wish to extol my skills and abilities here (my head is far to (sic) big already!!) but I know I was able to leave the Judge, DPP and Benjamin with a far better impression of First Bank than they initially had."

"I was also able to lay the way for an immediate judicial review of any decision made by the Attorney General in the event that he granted the FBI a search and seize warrant."

"Since my return I have had on-going discussions with the DPP and Benjamin in respect of the FBI and the foolishness of the FBI being given access to First."

He seemed just the man Van Brink wanted.

Jones also had further meetings with the government about establishing an autonomous "Freedom Zone" in Grenada for Brink and other dubious businessmen, the scheme which had already been floated before the prime minister's eyes. The Freedom Zone would effectively have created a state within a state and given businessmen additional protection from investigating authorities. Jones later claimed that he was trying to help sort out the mess and that it was he who was responsible for halting all new deposits into the bank, thus rendering the kiss of death to any Ponzi scheme.

In one letter, Jones discusses the setting up of structures outside Grenada to accept the bank's funds, which placed him in a precarious legal position since most of the bank's funds were already missing, a point of which he should have by now been aware. In another letter, he claimed to have met with Lloyd's of London underwriters about having FIBG insured by them, an unlikely scenario given FIBG's claimed annual interest rates of up to 250 per cent.

Still under pressure to provide an auditor, Lawrence Jones QC recruited an obscure accountant of his acquaintance from the northwest of England who in turn, even more bizarrely, engaged a garage proprietor from Middlesborough to carry out an assessment of the assets of First Bank. Adrian Ball and his unlikely assistant travelled to Grenada and set to work as others had before them to attempt to unravel the mysteries of First Bank. Anyway, they must have felt, they would get a trip to the Caribbean out of it if nothing else. The backgrounds of both men were obscure. Although a practising accountant with a clean record, Ball was not authorised to audit companies registered in his own country. His assistant, Derek Fowler, whom Ball does not seem to have known previously although from the same town, had a less than pristine record having been involved in an alleged scam involving High Yield Investment Programmes similar to those being promoted through First Bank

By the end of July Ball had delivered his report, still not in a form that could be recognised as a professional audit. It continued to list as assets the same nebulous bits of paper assigning these such as $47 billion worth of gold bullion held by Sherwood Investments in The Bahamas and various other unverifiable notes.

Much to the astonishment of those close to the heart of the matter, his report concluded that First Bank was solvent.

Meanwhile Jones felt that the only way he could make any sense out of the mess he had found was to recall Rita Regale back to Grenada. Although he distrusted her and felt that she had embezzled money on her own behalf, she was the only staff member left with any clues to be able to shed light on the murky organisation. She duly arrived to help—and was watched carefully during her entire visit.

In the Caribbean nations there exists a good deal of inertia in almost anything that needs decision making but finally the sleepy government of Grenada became sufficiently alarmed to rouse themselves to action of a sort. The Minister of Finance, Anthony Boatswain, who had taken over the post from the Prime Minister, finally appointed the former government auditor, Garvey Louison, to conduct an investigation into the affairs at First Bank and to assume control over it. First Bank responded by issuing a bulletin on its website:

August 17, 2000

> *The Government of Grenada has appointed someone to be on the inside of the bank to monitor its activity. This should not be construed as anything other than what it is…someone to monitor activity.*
>
> *IDIC is currently cooperating with various financial groups working at sorting out the primary problem, i.e., FB's inability to meet its obligations to its client banks and their depositors and FB's own direct depositor base.*
>
> *In the midst of this is the chaos caused by false allegations, innuendo, threats and the daily"news" that is promulgated by those who want to see the system fail.*
>
> *In a large sense, of course, the system has already failed. Failed, that is, to meet the expectations of depositors. Unfortunately there is no excuse for the fact that these expectations were based on the aggressive marketing tactics of those involved in promoting the various banks in the system.*
>
> *The question in the minds of those who still believe is, "When will the interest payments flow again?" To those who still believe, the answer is, based on some solid information from reliable sources, "Soon."*

To those who would prefer to make threats, call everyone involved "scam art-ists" (and worse)…the answer is: "It will happen when it happens."

Progress is being made. To those who believe, we say take comfort. To those who don't…no matter what is said…they will do what unbelievers do.

One way or another, depositors will eventually get what has been promised.

Are we saying that it is wrong to complain or doubt?

Of course not. Promises have been broken, obvious mismanagement has occurred. Complaining and doubting are both understandable—and certainly not unwarranted.

Please take the time, again, to carefully read the bulletin of August 11th below as well as the letter from the former CEO of FB and try to understand why more specific "news" is not forthcoming. For now, that is all we can pass along. We will continue to monitor the situation and update this web site with information that we feel can be reliably and safely revealed.

Five days later, Louison, seemingly unaware that he was only in place to "monitor" activities as FIBG claimed, since he signed himself "manager," opened the battle with a shot directly across the bows of the directors. In a letter adressed to "All Directors and Consultants to the Board of Directors and all Former Directors and Consultants to the Board", he spelled out his mandate. His third paragraph can have left little doubt in the minds of those addressed that things were going to get rough from now on.

"It is apparent that many millions of dollars have been transferred to Mr. Downes, Mr.and Mrs. Skirving and Mr. Van Brink either directly or through companies in which the aforesaid have or had a beneficial interest in, either directly or indi-rectly."

He noted that Certificates of Deposit had been issued for many millions of dollars without the funds appearing in the bank's account and that there were no tangible assets in place to cover such deposits. Furthermore he said he was aware that many millions of dollars had been transferred to Uganda and assets acquired there.

He asked for all information regarding all assets that they or their companies with which they were associated, either legally or beneficially, had acquired, add-ing that by all assets, he meant land, chattels and/or intangibles. In addition he required the original documents relating to the $62 billion claimed as assets of the bank. This last must have caused acute dyspepsia to an organisation previ-ously used to dealing only in photocopies.

They were given seven days to comply.

Since April, the bank had effectively ceased to function. Any monies received were immediately consumed for pressing local bills and no investors had been paid. The ship was firmly aground.

Worse was to follow as the crew abandoned ship.

David Springer, Barnabe's former accomplice and another Canadian, Peter Bean, were arrested attempting to board an aircraft at Port Salines airport as they tried to leave the country. They were charged with numerous offences including fraudulent breach of trust and conspiracy to defraud First Bank of substantial sums. That they were charged with stealing from First Bank, a corporate thief of some expertise, was an ironic twist. The police were also looking for Larry Barnabe but admitted that he had already escaped.

On the day that Louison took control, a group of investors, tired of promises that were never fulfilled, (they had already tried to cash in a CD without success) filed a Mareva Injunction against the bank. The Oxford Law Dictionary defines a Mareva Injunction thus:

> *An order of the court preventing the defendant from dealing with specified assets. Such an order will be granted in cases in which the plaintiff can show that there will be a substantial risk that any judgement given against the defendant will be worthless, because the defendant will sell assets to avoid paying it. It is usually granted to prevent assets leaving the jurisdiction of the English courts, but may in exceptional circumstances extend to assets abroad. It is named after the 1975 case Mareva Compania Naviera SA v International Bulkcarriers SA.*

The injunction was granted and a final nail hammered into First Bank's coffin.

"A thief believes everybody steals."

—E.W. Howe

19

A Falling Out of Thieves

Already mentioned has been the problems First Bank had in controlling the actions of its many sub-banks. Although these existed purely on paper and were administered effectively through the offices of FIBG, they continued to promote the fiction of independence.

The most successful of these was Crown Meridian Bank whose "Board of Directors" included Danny Hashimoto and Bruce Jeddeloh, both stalwarts from the operation in Maui. While Hashimoto seems to have been in Grenada, Jeddeloh was not, by this time having prudently decamped to Las Vegas, and, judging from their subsequent actions, they scarcely seemed to be speaking to each other. As pressure from depositors grew with the furore surrounding First Bank and its problems, they were both very much in the firing line, being the direct representatives with whom depositors had placed their trust and money.

Both were under intense pressure to respond to the increasingly fractious requests of depositors who had by now received no returns since April, and incredibly they elected to publish totally divergent statements concerning the position with Crown Meridian and its relationship with First Bank

By now Bruce Jeddeloh seemed to be having serious doubts concerning the future of both banks, his own Crown Meridian and First Bank. Although a devoted former acolyte of Van Brink, in the latter's absence his support seemed to be wavering and his letter to "his" clients (apparently it was not sent to all depositors at the bank) seemed to place the blame for the debacle firmly in the lap of Van Brink and First Bank, not at all the role that had been envisaged for a correspondent bank. It did, however, contain a good number of home truths, an unusual commodity in correspondence from any of First Bank's operatives. Much later, when all the dust had settled, Jeddeloh admitted privately that he knew that First Bank had been fraudulent from start to finish, but in this letter he chose to take the high moral ground.

His long and rambling exposition of "the truth", a popular phrase among First Bank associates, is reproduced in full, along with Danny Hashimoto's divergent statement, in Appendix B for those who wish to wade through it but depositors must have been both surprised and alarmed to receive, almost on the same day, the letter from Danny Hashimoto, the bank's other director, advocating a very different strategy for dealing with the problem. He appears to have confidence in First Bank's ability to surmount the difficulties and calls upon his clients to stand fast and to avoid putting pressure on First Bank and, inter alia, himself.

Where Jeddeloh proposes taking some sort of legal action, to be funded, naturally, by the already impoverished depositors, Hashimoto still pins his hopes upon the ephemereal power of IDIC, that non-existent entity, to resolve the problems and redeem investors. In view of his long association with Van Brink and Ferguson (he claims to have been the first to put down roots in Grenada) it is inconceivable that he could not have been fully aware of the true position and his letter can only be construed as a "playing for time" manouevre.

The confusion that receipt of these two divergent communications, both from so-called directors of their bank, must have engendered in the minds of their unfortunate clients can only be imagined, but were probably best expressed by a posting on a bulletin board from one of that increasingly confused number:

> "It should be apparent which one is confident, and which one wants to be responsible. Danny's letter indicates to me that he is neither a banker, nor a responsible businessman. He is confident, BELIEVES everything is gonna be just fine. He mentions some top consultants are working to achieve liquidity. Who are they? Why them? What are their credentials? We have been told these same worn out lame excuses for months, and nothing has transpired, yet for some reason we are expected a rabbit to pop out of the hat suddenly? This is insult upon insult to my limited intelligence.
>
> Danny: Where is the money? What are you doing, other than flapping your lips? You need to check in with Bruce. I am demanding that Crown Meridian Bank, and all responsible parties take action, and bring the truth to its depositors. And don't forget Danny, there is always alphabet soup. I suggest you start acting responsibly, and endorse bringing in Mr. Lundquist, or someone of his calibre. I would also suggest Lauriston Wilson.
>
> Forensic accountant? If these $60 billion in assets only exist in the imaginations of Gil Ziegler/Van Brink et al, then are we talking about some type of mind probe? Is this the reason Danny fears a forensic accountant?
>
> Or is it becaue the forensic accountant just might uncover the truth to the situation, and expose something that shouldn't be out in the open?
>
> Maybe he might discover that there just might have been fiduciary irresponsibility?"

Mismanagement of funds? Misallocation of funds? Fraud? Embezzlement? Possible criminal behavior?

Hmmmm, makes one wonder.

Good job Bruce, yer stepping in the right direction. Keep it up.

Speaking of IDIC, Van Brink pulls the proverbial rabbit out of the hat in his "I have subsequently learned that of the asset items you disparaged there has already been independent confirmation of several amounting to approximately US $5 billion."

Danny Hashimoto confirms the practices of FIBG as exposed by Michael Gabriel (Another outspoken critic of FIBG). The smoke and mirrors tactics and treatment of depositors like the enemy continues on. The usual lip service to those who press for answers.

my 2 bits.
Dirtdog."

In spite of all the words that flowed, threats that were made and promises that were broken, there was one unassailable fact at the end of it all—the money had long gone. First Bank did not have a bean to its name.

"Make money your god and it will plague you like the devil."

—Henry Fielding (1707–1754)

20

The Insurance Man Re-Surfaces

One of the factors that had persuaded a small group of investors in First Bank to apply for a Mareva Injunction was that, despite the claims that IDIC had insured them for 100% of their funds, IDIC was proving remarkably hard to pin down for them to be able to file their claim. Since being ejected from that most benevolent and relaxed of jurisdictions, Dominica, Douglas Ferguson and his mythical insurance company were lost in space as far as responding to any claims was concerned.

For all its boast of $20 million in assets, it seemed to be having a hard time finding a home where a telephone could be installed and was currently relying upon communication solely by way of a free Internet address at Hotmail and a website. Denied a home in any legitimate jurisdiction it was now referring to itself as "a West Indian Corporation," a completely meaningless title.

Suddenly, the elusive insurance provider sprang to life with an announcement on its website displaying an encouraging "News Flash" for depositors and a long-winded letter of protest to Mr. Louison:

September 11, 2000

BULLETIN

IDIC is currently working on a process to bring liquidity from bank-owned assets for the purpose of paying off all principal and interest due depositors. The following letter sent today is part of that process. IDIC is currently negotiating to set up a number of locations throughout the world to facilitate the claims process. Within 30 days, specific claims instructions will be posted on this web site. Please note, until that time, there will be no contact information available.

To get a full understanding of some of the undercurrent going on...please read the letter below:

Mr. Garvey Louison
Acting Manager
First International Bank of Grenada Limited
The Chester John Building
Young Street
St. George's, Grenada (West Indies)

Dear Mr. Louison:

We were monitoring the progress being made by the Bank's Board of Directors when you were appointed to make a special examination of the finances of the bank under conditions of secrecy by Grenada's Minister of Finance under section 20 of the Offshore Banking Act (1996). We have waited, now, for nearly a month following your appointment to have some sort of indication from you of your assessment of the financial status of the bank and have heard nothing.

As you are aware, the bank remains under contract to report all matters appertaining to any significant change in its asset structure to IDIC and that failure to do so is a breach of that contract and constitutes grounds for IDIC to step in and oversee the bank's operation for the benefit of depositor claims. Up until the date of your appointment the bank's board had been making significant progress toward remedying the bank's illiquid position through utilizing its assets obtained, in part, through joint venture agreements with various parties. Because of this measurable progress and the soon-scheduled successful conclusion of those matters, IDIC held off on triggering its rights under contract as to the protection of the bank's many depositors as well as the beneficial interests of its ownership.

If you will by writing assure IDIC that the depositors will receive all principal and interest accrued to date of settlement (within 60 days) with the preservation of the significant equitable interests of the bank's ownership, we will gladly post this news on our web-site for the benefit of the many depositors who query IDIC and regularly check on the bank's status.

IDIC has no desire to litigate any matter concerning the bank, nor does IDIC dispute the right of the Government of Grenada to step in and supervise the bank's operations at its discretion.

It troubles many depositors and the bank's ownership that since your appointment little progress seems to have been made (and perhaps much progress seems to have been stopped) toward bringing about a successful conclusion to this liquidity issue.

So far as we have been able to independently determine, you have retained the services of one of the Board's selected consultants from Europe to follow through on utilizing one of the joint venture assets (valued at US $3.8 billion) on behalf of the bank—and that you confirmed his appointment within hours or days of your appointment by the Minister of Finance. This is to your credit. No current report on this consultant's progress, however, is available to us, and it would seem that enough time has transpired that there would be a definitive answer from him and his large banking contacts in this regard.

What is perplexing to us (and to the bank's ownership and Board of Directors) is why you have not chosen to follow through on the placement of another of the bank's significant joint-venture assets (valued at US $855 million) into the profit producing program that had been negotiated by the Board as of the date of your appointment by the Minister of Finance.

Rather than quibble over what your office may have or may not have done in the one month since your 21-day special examiner's appointment began, we would propose that you execute, on behalf of First International Bank of Grenada, Limited, a Special Power of Attorney to IDIC as touching this US $855 million joint venture asset, so that IDIC may complete this negotiated, verified and confirmed transaction on behalf of the bank and its depositors.

As you know the bank's joint venture partner receives 50% of the income stream generated through utilization of this asset. The other 50% will be devoted to meeting depositor claims (less 10% for IDIC's fees and expenses). When all has been settled with the depositors, the balance of the income stream will revert to the benefit of the bank's other creditors and its ownership. Of course, should you have simultaneous success through the aforementioned consultant's initiatives, the situation will be resolved that much more quickly.

IDIC endured the board's reorganization in June and afforded it time to set these transactions in motion so that all depositors could quickly receive all of principal and interest due. We have hoped you would have by now finished these transactions and the issue would be moot, but the fact remains that there has been no official word from your office to the depositors as touching any-thing and the one official word you did release (by way of an open letter pub-lished in the media) was replete with errors, misconceptions and outright false allegations that anyone in possession of the facts would recognize. IDIC made no official comment as touching that letter, choosing instead to allow you the full 21 days of your appointment to adequately assess the situation and to make your final report. That 21 days has now fully passed with an extra week's grace period.

IDIC's role is to monitor and to move as and when it believes most prudent to do so on behalf of the bank's depositors. For the record, we estimate the total amount of principal and interest now owing the depositors is approximately US $360 million. This can be quickly liquidated in full on the basis of the various asset holdings the bank had acquired and through what the board had negoti-ated as of the time of your appointment. Any attempt on your part to now *assert that such full liquidation of depositor liabilities is not possible is unacceptable and we would fully protest, based on documents in the hands of counsel.*

Given this estimate and the time still necessary to bring all to a 100% settlement with depositors, IDIC now presents a claim of US $532 million to your administration of the bank. IDIC's claim precedes any other claim, as the contract between the bank and IDIC preceded the receipt of any deposit funds and was for the benefit of any depositors who would choose to do business with the bank. We do so now assert this claim to you, sir.

Again, IDIC does not seek confrontation with you or with Grenada's Ministry of Finance. Our intent, here, is to render the assistance we are called upon to perform, observing that you have let drop something we will gladly pick up and work to completion for the benefit of depositors, the bank's creditors, and the bank.

Yours truly,

Douglas C.Ferguson
Executive Director

It seems doubtful that this incredible farrago of nonsense was ever sent to Louison. It was intended merely as a sop to the frustrated investors to delay any further action by them and the wording (and length) carries the recognisable stamp of Van Brink. By now, all involved in the fiasco were well aware that the so-called assets of the bank were a chimera, otherwise they would have been liquidated long ago, and almost certainly it was common knowledge that IDIC was just another First Bank stooge. Also there was now the wonderful excuse that, due to the Mareva Injunction, the assets of First Bank that had been pledged to IDIC as security were now no longer available to be liquidated as promised. Therefore IDIC could no longer fulfil their part of the bargain. Game, Set, Match to IDIC.

If Louison did get a copy, it must have given him his only moment of amusement since moving into the office at First Bank. His research so far showed that the safe at First Bank would have a tough time coming up with $532 let alone with the $532 million demanded by IDIC on behalf of the depositors. The bulletin made no mention of the long silence from IDIC on the matter although depositors had made constant efforts to contact it since April, but the so-called insurer bargained for another thirty days grace by saying that no contact information would be available prior to then.

Ferguson also used another ploy to head off disgruntled customers. To one he wrote:

IDIC is following the prescription laid out for it in its contract with the bank. An apt analogy (albeit an oversimplification) follows.

A family is losing a loved one to the ravages of cancer and is watching him or her slowly lose the battle...while the medical expense and the anguish of the family grow. The doctors have already said "terminal" with only weeks or maybe months to live. The family may want to cry out for relief including from the insurance company that provided life insurance.

Does the company pay? Not until the patient is pronounced dead. The pronouncement of "terminal" doesn't do it. The cries of pain and anguish are understandable...the insurance company pays when the conditions of the contract are met. Death in that instance...this one is a bit more complicated...but the protection is there if all else fails...all else has not yet failed.

Douglas Ferguson most certainly did not believe that all else had failed as yet as far as he personally was concerned, although for the depositors he knew full well that it was a very different story. Mindful of his leader's discretion in taking flight, he prepared his own escape route.

To further baffle the depositors, IDIC published the following procedures for them to register any claims against First Bank. It includes the veiled threat, always presented by offshore scam artists, against disclosing any information that might trigger the tax authorities into taking an interest. This in itself was often enough to scare defrauded clients into keeping silent and not pursuing their claims.

> *The important thing to note at this moment is the process by which depositors will be able to receive what is due.*
>   *This bulletin is aimed at underscoring five things:*
>
> 1.   *Maintenance of absolute privacy and confidentiality through an encrypted process must be followed. Technology in this regard has advanced sufficiently to make the process developed for us only a few months ago obsolete. We are still several days away from completing the updated process.*
>
> 2.   *Destination of the funds once the actual claims process begins. Where funds are received can create problems of disastrous proportion...not only tax consequences, but also civil and even criminal penalties could ensue if improperly*

routed. Everyone should seek competent legal and tax counsel before they order funds sent.

3.   *The process that is being put in place over the next few days is **NOT** an actual claims process. YOU WILL BE GIVEN INSTRUCTIONS AS TO HOW TO COMPLETE AN **OUTLINE OF CLAIM** AND WHERE TO SEND IT. The purpose of this is to give depositors the opportunity to fulfill the requirements of arbitration language in the certificates of deposit. You will be asked to include any costs incurred to you because of the delays to interest payments or withdrawal demands. Late payment fees, any legal actions taken against you, loss of property and so on are just few examples of such costs. You will be given an e-mail contact address of the independent contractor claims processor as well as the arbitration advocate to answer any and all questions. SEND ALL QUESTIONS TO THAT GIVEN ADDRESS. We are told that it will be ready to post in just a few more days.*

4.   *Note that a third party under contract to IDIC will handle claims processing. That contractor will handle all inquiries and claims.*

5.   *IDIC recognizes and understands that this has been a lengthy and confusing process. IDIC recognizes and understands that many of you do not understand or agree with the strategy IDIC has chosen to follow over the past few weeks. The only response possible at this time is: IDIC had and has access to information about First Bank's problems that are not general knowledge. IDIC has a contractual, as well as a strategic, obligation to keep those details confidential. IDIC, the company and the people who comprise the company are deeply sympathetic and sorry for the pain, loss, frustration, disappointment, and confusion over the course of this situation. Whether you choose to believe it or not is your decision, but IDIC has acted and will continue to act in a manner it believes will best serve the depositors. When this crisis has come to resolution, IDIC may be in a position to share more information that will fill in the gaps for some of you.*

6.   *However, until that time, we ask that you believe that IDIC is acting in a manner it believes will ultimately serve your best interests and help the process by filling out an initial claims outline and supporting documentation. If you feel you cannot do that, we ask that you at least not hinder the process by flooding IDIC with questions we simply cannot answer at this time.*

Please watch this space for updates.

Yet another sop to keep investors quiet, it is notable mainly for the number of words taken to tell them precisely nothing, except to sit, wait and, most importantly, to keep quiet. The request not to flood the company with questions was very relevant since IDIC only had one staff member, Mr. Douglas C. Ferguson himself and no recognised fixed abode. In addition, as Hotmail users well know, there is a limit to the number of messages that can be stored in the "in-box." Not surprisingly, the address and identity of the impressively titled "independent contractor claims processor" never did appear on the website which also seemed to disappear sporadically for reasons unknown.

Meanwhile, politics, never far in the background in The Caribbean, reared its ugly head.

"Politics is the art of looking for trouble, finding it whether it exists or not, diagnosing it incorrectly, and applying the wrong remedy."

—Ernest Benn

21

The Prime Minister Acts

Being the head of government in a country with a population 100,000 is more akin to being mayor of a decent sized town elsewhere. Being a nation does, however, attract rather more attention in the international field that events say, for instance, in Podunk IL or Durkeyville IN, usually arouse.

For some months Prime Minister Mitchell had been only too aware that the golden glow of offshore banking in which he had been basking was likely to turn itself into some rather unpleasant dross at any moment. Lawsuits were beginning to descend upon Grenada, the most prominent being filed by a group of depositors from something called Investors International, an organization based in Switzerland that claimed to have more than 800 members who invested a total of $69 million in First Bank and various companies associated with it. The suit sought $1.965 billion in damages, rather dwarfing Grenada's annual budget. The media were gleefully looking forward to more scandalous revelations and David Marchant just would not shut up. Ever since his troubling conversation with Lauriston Wilson, Mitchell realised what he had probably always known, that First Bank was completely, utterly and irretrievably fraudulent.

Despite his protestations of innocence, his political party had accepted donations from the bank and many party members as well as local businessmen had benefited directly and indirectly from Van Brink's generosity. Generosity is a fairly cheap commodity when you are using someone else's money and Van Brink had spread it around like golden manure. Now the end, if not in sight, was clearly just over the horizon.

Shortly before Brink's precipitate departure, Robert Skirving had sent a memo to him, copied to Mark Kennedy and Douglas Ferguson, and headed "A Few Ideas."

He starts by proposing that they license a new bank in Grenada to take over all of First Bank's assets, "like we did with Fidelity," he says. "We can then start fresh as far as an audited financial statement is concerned." There is then some vague mention of revenue for the bank coming from the Legacy/Hope pro-gramme, presumably another investment scam, and from unspecified gold and precious metal projects that may be a reference to Brink's dealings in the Congo.

He then discusses sending Rita Regale to Palau to set up a new bank there and suggests First Bank of the Pacific as being a good name.

Then, "I would like it if Van, Doug, Mark and myself discuss and pray about internal issues and possible solutions to those issues before meeting with the rest of the board. This does not mean that we cover up or not share things with the board, I just think we could save a lot of time and maybe avoid future problems from occurring if we could pray about certain sensitive information before shar-ing it with others." It seems doubtful that the prayer meeting was ever convened and the Almighty's advice taken, since Van Brink was en route to Kampala a few days later. Or maybe that was the Almighty's advice.

The memo must have planted the seed of an idea for, as the First International Bank of Grenada spiralled into oblivion, a new First Bank was rising like a fiscal phoenix, magically transformed into First Bank of Grenada 2000 Ltd. with the blessing of the government of Grenada. An announcement headed "Recovery Plan" went to all the depositors:

OUTLINE OF RECOVERY PLAN

A company styled First International Bank of Grenada (2000) Ltd. has been established. After satisfying himself that the capitalisation requirements as set in the Act have been met, the Minister of Finance has granted the said Company a Class 1 banking license.

Pursuant to the powers of the Minister, the license to First International Bank of Grenada 2000 Ltd. has been granted on the following conditions:

Within a reasonable period of time cause all legitimate depositors to either receive their legitimate deposits paid to First International Bank of Grenada (FIBG) or give the said depositors the option to convert their said deposits to a new form of deposit or investment upon terms to be agreed and backed by a certificate of deposit, lawfully issued by the licensee of such security as may be deemed appropri-ate by the depositor. The Licensee may for the purpose of calculating the sum to be returned to the said depositors take into consideration such sums of money that may have already been paid to the respective depositors or a third party on the depositors instructions;

Ensure that the Directors of FIBG 2000 Ltd. are actively involved in the oper-ations of the Bank and that all banking activity is properly supervised;

Appoint a qualified person in the field of accountancy to, inter alia, ensure proper records are kept and all times.

In view of the total lack of funds in First Bank's vaults, the adequate capitalisation referred to had to be taken with a grain of salt (presumably more photocopies had been provided) and a sign of the desperation felt by the government to bolster an already failing industry.

Prime Minister Mitchell's extraordinary decision to try and postpone the inevitable was seen by victims as further proof that his government had no intention of taking any positive action. "It is clear that this new bank is being formed with the money that has been stolen from depositors of the first bank," said a depositor.

"If First Bank 2000 Ltd. is allowed to begin operations, then we will have little choice but to take legal action against Mitchell and any other government official who is in any way implicated in this scandal."

At a press conference, the government announced that FIBG owed at least $150 million (a grave under estimate) but said that a condition of the new license was that the liabilities of FIBG must be honoured but giving no indication as to how this was to be achieved. Significantly, a more compliant government employee, Errol Thomas, replaced Louison, who had asked a number of embarrassingly pertinent questions regarding the bank's dubious asset status. One of Mitchell's ongoing problems was that in his capacity as Minister for Information in Grenada, he had frequently trumpeted the success of First Bank in official announcements and had thus deluded many into pouring more funds into it, making him very much a party to any potential lawsuits that now seemed to be inevitable.

Most observers treated the announcement of the new bank with disbelief and viewed it as an attempt by the Grenada government to delay impending political disaster from the scandal, which was the only construction that could be put upon it. Clearly visions of Monserrat were dancing in Mitchell's head when he made the incredible decision to licence yet another fraudulent operation to boost the status of the more than eighteen already existing ones.

Mitchell did not respond to a list of questions sent to him by David Marchant of Offshore Alert, still hot on the trail, one of which asked why a bona fide new bank would agree to honour another institution's debts. Being unanswerable, Mitchell wisely left it that way.

And then, out of the blue, Douglas Ferguson decided he had had enough and elected to retire. Tired of being the nominal head of a non-existent insurance company in cyberspace, he performed what might have seemed the well-nigh impossible trick of "selling" IDIC—but the purchaser was to be none other than the man whose brainchild it had been in the first place, Van Brink. As the only means of communication for the homeless company seems to have been the Internet, the announcement duly appeared on the IDIC website.

Dec. 6, 2000

IDIC IS PURCHASED BY UGANDAN INVESTOR GROUP

International Deposit Indemnity Corporation (IDIC) has been purchased by an investor group based in Kampala, Uganda. The announcement of the take-over was made today in a joint statement released today by IDIC and by Union Capital Fund, a Kampala-based investment fund for which Van Brink, former Chairman of the Board and CEO of First International Bank of Grenada, now serves as an international consultant and contracted spokesman.

When asked about the reasons for his involvement in the acquisition of the much-criticized IDIC, Brink stated, "From a personal standpoint, it makes total sense. There have been those who have alleged that IDIC was nothing but a scam and a Van Brink alter ego. No amount of proof and assertion of the facts to the contrary made that allegation go away. I was able to demonstrate to the directors of UCF the total long-term viability of IDIC and its worthiness as an investment. It's as simple as that," he said.

IDIC is the contracted third-party administrator of the self-insurance program for First International Bank of Grenada (First Bank), a bank that fell on hard times several months after Brink resigned with rumors widely-quoted in the press that he had made off with millions or billions in bank funds, rumors he has insisted are groundless.

"What better way to defend IDIC's viability and to vindicate myself than for me to personally become involved?" Brink asked. "I had nothing previous to do with IDIC's management. It was and is an arms-length relationship, enforced by contract and by the trust that managed IDIC", he added.

Much has been made about the close personal relationship between Brink and IDIC's Executive Director as "proof" of some sort of common ownership and collusion. Brink had but two words to say on that topic, "Utter nonsense."

Brink has long acknowledged that having an asset-based mechanism to protect depositors was his "brainchild" but adds that how the program evolved and was administered was often against his personal desires and judgment while he was CEO of First Bank, IDIC's largest client.

IDIC's retiring Executive Director, Douglas Ferguson, concurred in that assessment, stating that from time to time Brink "did attempt to tell IDIC how to operate its business and on some of those occasions he was told, not always politely, to mind his own business."

Ferguson explained that since the bank's contract with IDIC dictated the relationship there was little Brink could do, but "sit down and shut up", although he

*never seemed to do so without argument, Ferguson noted. "Sometimes his argu-
ments were taken into consideration, but not because of any control or ownership,"
he said, wryly adding that in spite of all that has been written about him, on occasion Brink was capable of actually demonstrating sound business judgment.*

*Brink said, "It gives me a deep sense of satisfaction to now have the opportunity
to have a close working involvement with IDIC being the vehicle to make financially whole all the depositors in First Bank and its client institutions."*

*A specific part of the negotiations with UCF was that IDIC existing Executive
Director's wish to retire would be honored. Ferguson, however, has agreed to
maintain an advisory role to the new Board of Directors, but will no longer be an
integral part of IDIC's management.*

*As to questions about who Ferguson's successor will be and whether the corpo-
rate name will be changed, Brink stated that UCF is considering several viable
options. "The one thing on everyone's mind is to get things resolved as quickly as
possible in favor of the depositors," he said.*

*Brink was asked if this action would set off another flurry of allegations in the
press as to his "presumed ownership" of IDIC. "I cannot be responsible for what the
press does. With respect to myself, to First Bank or to IDIC, the press has consis-
tently demonstrated a profound disinterest in truth and seems to prefer sensational-
ism to fact," he said.*

*For the time being IDIC, or its differently named successor, will continue to
make announcements through IDIC's web site.*

*IDIC is pursuing a binding arbitration against First Bank on behalf of all
depositors and other creditors, Brink said, adding that "the viability of IDIC's case
and the certainty of First Bank's base of useable assets is what persuaded UCF to
make the purchase offer."*

*Brink said he thinks that perhaps some depositors will see this as an attempted
"cover-up" on his part, while most, he said, would probably view this as the most
hopeful news they have had in some months. "The fact is that I am neither a villain needing to cover the tracks of any wrong-doing, nor am I the messiah of
money," Brink said. "The acquisition is a viable move for UCF and infuses IDIC
with the essential independent resources it needs to complete its mission on behalf of
the depositors of First Bank and its client banks."*

As full of untruths and distortions as were most of First Bank's statements, it is
unlikely depositors took much comfort from the fact that Van Brink was now
officially recognised as the head of IDIC or from the fact that it was now conveniently re-located in Uganda. The sale was, of course, a complete and utter sham,
yet another tactic to delay action by depositors to take legal action to recover their
money.

The purchasing entity seems to have been as nebulous a body as IDIC had
ever been and the announcement discreetly failed to reveal any contact information for the new offices in Kampala. Clients were still stuck with a Hotmail

address to keep in touch with their insurance company. And, naturally, Van Brink was only involved as "an advisor and spokesman," the same role he was to enjoy with First Bank 2000.

22

The Bank that Never Was

The new bank started life under a distinctly disadvantageous financial cloud. With its licence conditional on making good the debts of First Bank, with First Bank's assets, such as they were, frozen by the Mareva Injunction, no money in the kitty and with no new investments arriving, there was no conceivable way in which operations could begin. Most of the staff, unpaid for some time now, had left and only the visionary Van Brink in faroff Kampala was still enthusiastic and buoyant as ever. Having once resigned for the good of the bank he was now back in the picture as an unpaid (sic) consultant for the good of the bank. Never at a loss for words, he later gave his own version of events following the departure of Louison and the investiture of Errol Thomas in his place, who it was felt would be more cooperative:

> *"At this development we all had high hopes that common sense would start prevailing in Grenada. We could not imagine that Grenada didn't want to see the rescue of the bank and its thousands of system depositors.*
>
> *One of the Board's members (Richard Downes) then finalized negotiations to result in $1.1 billion worth of income to the bank over the coming year (beginning November 2000). All that was needed was for First Bank to make standard bank-to-bank acknowledgements in a timely manner and to declare to what banking coordinates it wished the income to be sent.*
>
> *Mr. Thomas failed to respond on a timely basis, saying that he had to have direct authorization by the Minister of Finance to proceed. That offer of $1.1 billion in income for First Bank died on the table, with the parties on the income-producing side of things quite upset over their wasted time and energy on the bank's behalf.*
>
> *Hearing this, I prevailed upon a respected Grenadian to intervene personally with the Minister of Finance and to obtain for Mr. Thomas the Minister's consent to the financial restoration of the bank. That consent obtained, Richard Downes then went back to the party prepared to produce the income for the bank to reestablish that offer. That party couldn't do so through the former sources utilized, so*

turned to other sources. The offer was put forward again in the first few days of January 2001.

This time, Mr. Thomas said it was impossible for him to make the standard bank-to-bank acknowledgments, since there remained no one on bank staff who knew how to operate the bank's telex machine. Rather than call in a former First Bank employee for 15 minutes work, a few days later (January 12, 2001) Mr. Thomas marched into court to present a petition on behalf of the Minister of Finance that First Bank should be put to involuntary liquidation and that the firm that the government had retained several months previously as First Bank's auditors (PriceWaterhouseCoopers) should be named by the court as being the bank's Liquidator.

At (or perhaps without regard to) my urging, First Bank's legal ownership, First Bank's Board of Directors, IDIC and many, many depositors protested this action by writing directly to the court. The court set aside all such protests and on February 28, 2001, issued the order for involuntary liquidation of the bank and named PriceWaterhouseCoopers as Liquidator of First Bank."

It would have made more interesting reading if the identity of the mysterious investor with $1.1 billion to burn had been made known or a few details of the source of this staggering income revealed to Mr. Thomas and his government. It was probably a reference to two loan applications that Downes had made in June. The first, on 5th. June, was for $3,800,000,000 addressed to the G.E.P. International Group in Malaysia. This was to have been for a five-year term and to have been used "mainly for humanitarian projects in the G77 countries". The collateral offered was the two Dai-Ichi Kangyo post-dated cheques, whose validity had already been discounted by the FBI. Perhaps thinking that the requested amount had been too modest, a second loan request was made to the same group on the 17th.of June for $21.6 billion, this time the collateral offered being "top-rated, cash equivalent instruments that have been deeded to First Bank in an amount equal to the face value of the loan." The diverse list of projects for which these funds were said to be needed included a Free Trade Zone and a private school in Uganda, a private university in St. Kitts, a buffalo ranch in Canada and the "Dream Family Network", whatever that might have been, in Great Britain. This request was graced by the signature, not only of Downes but also by that of Robert E. Skirving.

Whilst the G.E.P. Group might have been forgiven for asking why First Bank did not simply liquidate their cash equivalent instruments and save themselves a lot of interest, it is more likely that, even in far away Malaysia, word had gotten around concerning First Bank and its activities. There appears to have been no response to the applications

As it was, still conscious of having been fooled by too many photocopies in the past, The Government of Grenada this time wisely decided it was time to end the pantomime.

The winding up petition is revealing. It states that, "No Director, Shareholder or Agent of First Bank resides or are present in Grenada. Furthermore, their whereabouts are not known. Therefore it is not proposed to serve this petition on any party." The petition lists the principal indebtedness as $206,467,938 with outstanding interest owed at $266,532,062. Local debts were listed as being $197,965. From this it was clear that First Bank of Grenada 2000 Ltd. had never made it to the starting post. Price Waterhouse were recommended to carry out the liquidation, a decision that had to be reversed when it was found that they were not technically eligible, having been previously engaged as auditors and the job requiring an individual be appointed. One of the partners was thus selected for this thankless task and Marcus Wide found himself in the job.

And so The First International Bank of Grenada disappeared, unmourned by the legitimate financial community but sadly missed by the many who had been deluded into placing their trust and their savings into the pockets of Van Brink and his associates.

And eight days later, Van Brink got married to Annet Asiimwe in Kampala—which is where we came in.

"You can fool some of the people all the time, and all of the people some of the time, but you cannot fool all of the people all the time."

—**Abraham Lincoln**

23

The Melody Lingers On

Conventionally, this should have been the end of the story and Van Brink would have remained in private and connubial bliss in Kampala, undisturbed by indignant defrauded depositors whilst the liquidator went about his business to see what could be recovered from the carnage left behind.

But that would have been to underestimate Brink.

Since Price Waterhouse had been involved with the dying days of First Bank, Marcus Wide must have had a pretty good insight into what he might expect to find once he got to grips with the situation. His first report arived in the commendably short time of a month and contained little to gladden the hearts of any depositors or creditors. To no-one's surprise, he had established that the assets of the bank were totally fraudulent and, equally unsurprisingly, that there was no money in the kitty. He included a request for a meeting with the past and present directors of the bank to discuss his findings, offering to pay their travel expenses to do so. It would have been a marvellous party—but nobody showed up.

The lesser perpetrators of this massive fraud had by this time all left for their home territories and were busy maintaining a low profile. However, the creator of this most fraudulent of banking enterprises, remained very much in the limelight, courtesy of the Internet. Many of the unfortunates who had swum with the First Bank tide were computer savvy and it was only a matter of time before bulletin boards started to appear on the Internet, mounted by aggrieved depositors, discussing their woes and possible means of recourse. One such was called "Inside Scoop" and sub-titled, "The real story of The First Bank of Grenada." Hosted by one signing himself, Ira M. Samuels, this purported to be working assiduously to recover the funds apparently missing from First Bank records. Pledging to "Get Our Money," the site propounded a number of possible options for creditors, all of which required them to contribute to a "Recovery Fund." American River Tax Consultants at 8041 Greenbank Lane in Citrus Heights, CA 95610 supposedly administered this fund. The message board also provided a platform for Van

Brink to expound upon the problems at the bank, problems which he insisted, at great length, were purely created by the government, the accountants and, in particular, Mr. Wide, the liquidator and David Marchant of Offshore Alert.

In some of his more bizarre outpourings, he claims that First Bank had been in fine order when he left and that the missing funds had been somehow snaffled by the managers, staff, government and/or Mr. Wide, you could take your pick. Marcus Wide produced three reports on affairs at First Bank, each one more depressing than the last, and Van Brink, in spite of the delights of his new matrimonial position, found the time to publish long and boring, point by point rebuttals of doubtful validity on the bulletin boards.

From time to time, Ira Samuels would post almost equally long missives reporting on the progress (or lack of it) being made and bemoan the slow way in which funds were being paid into the recovery fund. Since Mr. Samuels posted under an admitted pseudonym and since, in many respects, his writing style bore a strange resemblance to that of Van Brink, there were some who were churlish enough to believe that they might be one and the same person. Just before Labour Day he reported:

From: *"Ira M. Samuels"* <*getreal20012002@y...*>
Date: *Fri Aug 30, 2002 11:43 am*
Subject: *Legal Fund Report: 30 August 2002*

Minimum Goal: US $50,000.00.
Receipts to Date: $31,770.00
Amount Still to Raise: $18,230.00
Notes:

Three parties sending in funds sent them in via personal check rather than in the form of a money order. We will go ahead and deposit these checks and hope that no problems arise in collecting upon them.

Please—Send funds in the form of a money order.

For those who have yet to make a pledge, send that by e-mail to: volunteerfinance @ yahoo. com

Please DO NOT send in pledge funds if you have not sent in an e-mail telling about your pledge. Again, e-mail pledges need to be directed to: volunteerfinance @ yahoo. com

If you HAVE made a pledge but have lost the instructions on where to send the funds (or never received the instructions originally), also write to: volunteerfinance @ yahoo. com

The Executive Committee has been hard at work on several details—almost 130 e-mails back and forth on various matters this week alone among the various committee members, including further questions to answer for prospective legal counsel and on miscellaneous lawsuit organizational details.

Those of you in the United States are heading into the traditional Labor Day Holiday weekend—a celebration of recognizing that the workman is worthy of his hire and saluting those who do work.

No member of the executive committee will be paid for having served on the committee. But if you had any idea of the thousands of pages of reading and commenting, strategizing, questioning and answering that has gone on weekly at the Executive Committee for the past fifteen months, you would appreciate (as I do) what workmen each of them are. I wish each of those Americans on the committee (and all American members of our extended Getthemoney group) a relaxing, rejuvinating Labor Day!

Kind Regards,

Ira

Mr. Samuels gives no clue as to the indentity of the "executive committee" who were working so hard to retrieve, what must have been apparent to any reasonable person, funds that no longer existed. He refused the liquidator's request to reveal his own identity, Ira Samuels name does not appear in the records of First Bank nor any of its sub-banks, and the true purpose of the fund remains something of an enigma. One exotic scheme involved suing the liquidators, Marcus Wide, Price Waterhouse and the Government of Grenada for mis-appropriating the funds of First Bank, an extraordinary premise but in keeping with the tenor of accusations that appear on the board.

Brink's self-justificational messages on this board (and there are several hundred of them, almost all lengthy) are so extreme and at variance with the established facts that it could almost be attributed to some sort of mental abberation and a refusal to accept that his activities, almost from day one, had been fraudulent. He seems to have become a victim of his own criminal imagination and it is difficult to understand why he continued, voluntarily, to stay in the public eye when he might well have retired quietly with his ill-gotten gains in Uganda. Perhaps the answer lies in just how long ill gotten gains last when one is hiding out.

Historically, not for too long and it is conceivable that proceeds from the "Recovery Fund", although disappointingly skimpy as Mr. Samuels reported, might be buying a few rounds of drinks at the Rhino Bar in Kampala. Already Uganda was proving an unwilling and reluctant host to him, in spite of his marriage, as a local paper reported:

> *Conman On The Run*
> *A MAJOR international conman has taken up residence in Uganda. Van Brink, formerly Gilbert Allen Ziegler, is now living in an Mbuya mansion. He is also believed to be the owner of Capetown Villas and two warehouses in Kampala. Until last year Van Brink was the chief executive of the First International Bank of Grenada that has now gone into receivership. The liquidator from PricewaterhouseCoopers estimates that over $200 million of depositor's funds have gone missing while he has so far only recovered around $300,000. Some estimates say that Van Brink may have benefited by over $30 million from his involvement in FIBG. Van Brink is a master spin-doctor who claims that he has been a victim of a conspiracy. The brutal reality is that Van Brink ripped off the life savings of many American depositors who were foolish enough to believe that the FIBG could pay them 100% interest year after year. Uganda does not need any more bad publicity yet Van Brink is about to drag Uganda into the mud yet again. Soon the Grenada government will start trying to recover the assets that vanished with Van Brink and his friends. There will be subpoenas and claims on Ugandan banks and properties. To make matters worse, there is a strong possibility that Van Brink may face criminal proceedings for his extradition to the USA or Grenada. All his will all be reported in the international media. Van Brink has been carefully constructing himself a comfortable nest in Kampala complete with a Ugandan wife and high-level contacts. But is he the kind of person that Uganda should give shelter to?*

No doubt the only way in which Van Brink could survive would be by a process, familiar to anyone who has lived in such places, of discreet bribery of government officials, a policy that has a deleterious effect on the largest of nest eggs. His comfort level would not have been much improved when the local paper, New Vision, published the following report of the liquidator's third publication:

> *First International Bank of Grenada founder Van Brink stripped $4.5 million of assets out of the bank not long before it went bust, according to its liquidator.*
> *In his third report to creditors dated June 1, 2002, Marcus A. Wide, of PriceWaterhouseCoopers, reported that details of the asset transfers were contained "unsigned minutes from FIBG's June 2000 Board of Directors meeting."*
> *The minutes indicated that "depositor funds of approximately $4.5 million" were transferred to several companies "owned and/or controlled" by FIBG founder Van Brink (a.k.a. Gilbert Ziegler) in Uganda where he now lives.*

These included a house complex at Mbuya Hill, Kampala, at a cost of US$1,300,000; shares in Kampala Lakeside Resort Beach Ltd., US$2,000,000; shares in Nsimbe Ideal Home, US$450,000 and an advance to the African Union Reserve System, US$800,000.

"It is the position of the Liquidator that the transfer of the Uganda Assets to companies owned and/or controlled by Mr. Brink on the eve of the insolvency of the Bank was illegal, and constitutes a fraudulent settlement, a fraudulent preference, and a related party transaction," reported Wide.

Eighteen months after FIBG went into liquidation in Grenada, no one has yet been criminally charged in relation to the fraud, which constituted one of the biggest in the history of offshore finance.

Wide stated that he has been pursuing action to have his status as FIBG's liquidator recognised in Uganda, where some of the bank's assets, as well as its former principal, Van Brink, are located.

"After an intensive effort by my legal counsel in Uganda, I was advised on May 15, 2002 that the Uganda Minister has issued the necessary orders enabling the recognition of my Grenada appointment in Uganda."

"The Statutory Orders have been prepared and will be retroactive from the date of my appointment in Grenada, February 28, 2002."

"I am advised that this means I will be able to review and potentially set aside any dealing with the assets that have occurred in the interim."

"The assets improperly held in Uganda are also proceeds of crime, which itself creates possible remedies. I am now in the process of seeking assistance from the courts in Uganda to recover the Uganda Assets. However, my counsel has advised that while I should be able to recover the assets, it will be a difficult and time-consuming process."

In his report, Wide again warned creditors that there may not be a dividend distribution.

He advised "there is a real and distinct possibility that there will be no distribution whatsoever made by the Liquidator to the FIBG depositors/creditors".

Wide forecast that "total gross realisations in respect of the FIBG assets could be as low as $1.6 million"—a tiny figure compared with the bank's estimated liabilities at liquidation of US$473 million.

FIBG is so broke that there is not even enough to pay liquidation fees, reported Wide.

At May 31, 2002, the liquidator had available funds of just $6,009 and held unpaid invoices of $175,000 owed for legal fees and $325,000 owed to the liquidator.

"As set out in detail in my First Report and Second Report, the information and evidence before me has led me to the conclusion that FIBG was a sham from its inception, that there was no intention to provide the yields offered, nor to return money to depositors beyond the 'Ponzi' component of making payment to some depositors to encourage others, that potential depositors were subject to fraudulent misrepresentation with respect to the potential investment opportunities offered by FIBG, stated Wide".

Despite all the efforts of Marcus Wide and law enforcement authorities, Van Brink remains at large in Uganda and, apparently flourishing. There are reports that he moved into a new house. One such read: *"Runaway banker Van Brink has moved into a new plush house that he has bought in Luzira. I hear he still has his Mbuya complex with two houses, a giant swimming pool and squash court, but it is now rented out to officials from the EU and UTL. And who said****does not pay?*

And even though the liquidator has obtained permission to pursue assets in Uganda, there is little guarantee of his having much success, as long as Van Brink can come up with the payoffs.

Justice has, however, caught up with a few of the lesser lights. John Brinker and Gary Bentz, bosses of Wellington Bank and Trust together with David Rowe of Cambridge International Bank have all been indicted on various charges but many others are still out there, lost, but, it is to be hoped, not forgotten.

Richard Downes returned to his home in Suffolk, Canada where he refuses to speak of his tenure at the bank, on the advice of his lawyers, he claims, and Robert Skirving's Bank of Nations, a pale shadow of First International, failed miserably, causing him to file for bankruptcy. Neither has so far been charged with any wrongdoing. Mark Kennedy went home to Canada, apparently with a letter from First Bank absolving him of any wrongdoing and Lawrence Jones once again donned his wig and robe in London. Adrian Ball returned to his Middlesborough UK practice where he has an unlisted phone number.

Tannsen Sumeru, deciding that spiritual discretion was the better part of valour, gave up his home in Santa Barbara and said he was "going traveling," planning to visit a series of "spiritual communities" around the world in hopes of finding one where he would settle and preferably one where they had not heard of The Bank of World Peace.

Mitchell survived the political fallout and remained Prime Minister of Grenada, albeit with a drastically reduced banking portfolio, all of FIBG's correspondent banks having lost their licences. Michael Creft resigned, still protesting his innocence and claiming that he was suffering from hair loss as a result of the stress of his job.

Incredibly, some depositors still held out hopes of recovery, hopes that were fed by the dis-information continuing to be spread by Van Brink and his flying fingers at the computer keyboard. They never seemed to rest.

Some benighted souls still contributed to the so-called recovery fund when it had been conclusively proved that there was less than nothing to recover, but presumably they were happy in making a continuing contribution to the Brink Benevolent Fund.

Then early 2003, Ira Samuels posted a startling message on his board:

"IT'S OVER!!

Our FUNDRAISING DRIVE is over.

Based on e-mails we have received from contributors who have indicated they have mailed in contributions-and based on contributions received already this week, we are finished with fundraising. As always, full details on receipts and expenditures will be posted to each who have made contributions.

If you have been sitting by waiting to see more involvement by others before you make a contribution to our effort, you are now too late to lend a hand.

What happens now that we have met our fundraising goal?

First, we wait for the engaged asset recovery firm to meet its goal.

Anticipated is $2 million to $12 million in initial recoveries.

When those recoveries are received, we will then award bonuses to those who have contributed to the effort—bonuses ranging from 2:1 to 10:1 on the amount contributed (depending upon how much was contributed). AFTER pay-ing out the scheduled bonuses to contributors, the Executive Committee will establish a "reserve fund" for legal expenses. This is so that we NEVER-EVER have to ask for contributions again. The Committee, once again, will be seeking to engage the most competent law firm available to undertake our case—then engage them and let them go ahead and do their job. The Committee will pro-vide such back-up and claimant organizational services as we can offer. We anticipate that more than enough will be recovered to pay all bonuses AND to engage a solid law firm well capable of undertaking our complex case.

This brings us down to what to do with what we believe will be the excess in recoveries over and above these initial funds commitments.

Here are the options, as we see it:

1.   Invest a portion in additional recovery efforts.

2.   Reserve some contingency funds for the assisting in back-up and claimant organizational services that will be necessary.

3.   Distribute the remainder on a pro-rata basis to all who have contributed (in proportion to the amounts they have contributed).

4. Distribute the remainder evenly divided among all who have contributed (without regard to the amounts each have contributed).

5. Distribute the remainder on a pro-rata basis among all who have pre-registered claims with our group (whether they have contributed having no bearing on eligibility).

6. Create a distribution formula that incorporates elements of each of the above-devoting a percentage of excess funds to each of the five above categories.

Personally, I like option 6.

I recognize that beyond receiving the scheduled bonuses, absolutely NOTHING would have happened, if those who did contribute had not stepped forward in faith and commitment to see our fundraising goal met. So beyond bonus consideration (that was available to any and all who chose to contribute—and available to those who chose NOT to contribute, as well), members of "The Atlas Club" (those who DID contribute) deserve some sort of priority consideration.

Take, for instance, the below quotation from one of multiple depositors who individually contributed several thousand dollars each in the past week.

BEGIN QUOTE:

Ira,

I don't think that any of us really understood how much it would cost the group to not meet the deadline. I stood by hoping that everyone would do their parts. Being a very small investor in Crown Meridian, I did the minimum $50, and then another $100 as time passed (and I was able to save up), and thought I had done my part to go the extra mile that all of the committed were willing to stretch for to get the job done. However, by the emails, it appears that this was not enough.

Yesterday, I sent off all the cash I could scrounge up ($650) to hit the $800 that would give me the ultimate bonus. However, in looking at the whole picture, and after some reflection, I realized that I had invested everything at one time to Crown Meridian because I had faith in Danny and Van, and I now feel I should put it all out there once again since both of these individuals have shown guts beyond anyone else I've known to try to make things right. As I have listened to your handling of the situation month after month, and have seen your persistence and sensed your integrity, I now see three people who I *believe are on the right track and want to do everything possible to rectify our situation.*

Believe me, I am only a very small fry compared to a lot of the other investors, but since I put everything on the line once, I guess I'm willing to do it again, hoping that my retirement is still out there. I have borrowed enough from friends and family to put money in an account that I feel certain I can obtain a cashier's check from tomorrow that will meet our goal by our deadline.

Assuming that the others pledging the $5,500 come through, and other people inspired by the recent shock of another 5% out the window will respond with "something," I'm hoping that I can send in $X,XXX and have our goal met by the deadline. I am going to get the check in the morning and do not anticipate any hang-ups, but I have known banking establishments to Pull off all sorts of tricks at the last minute to delay "done deals." I have the money in a [name of brokerage] Money Market account that "should be" liquid. Therefore, I send this email with caution, but with great expectation that we have this financial situation solved. AND, if the $X,XXX is not enough, I will be able to fill the gap between what has been raised and what is left owing, but want to leave an opening for those who still want to come on-board to receive the generous bonuses. (I have the full amount needed) I would love to receive all the bonuses available, but am out on a long limb of faith here and will be very happy with the amount that bridging the gap will bring.

I will send you an email as soon as I put the cashier's check in the mail. Please do not post this until it is a "done" deal. I hope you understand my caution. The money is there; it's good as gold, but I'm sure you've been around the block a time or two yourself and understand my caution. So forget about people making loans to the group at insanely high interest rates. I think we are beyond that. Hopefully, we can get all this transacted well ahead of the deadline and relax into our prosperity. I look forward to sending you good news tomorrow. END QUOTE.

Even though by this individual's request we didn't post the message sent, from the day we received notice of the intended contribution, the entire energy and spirit of contributors seemed to shift—with momentum to complete, absolute accomplishment rather than to complaining about others who hadn't contributed anything at all.

That writer, in my opinion, SPOKE THE REAL TRUTH. When we originally made deposits into the FIBG system, each of us did so IN A SPIRIT OF FAITH and full commitment. How, then, could we think to come out of this and recover in a spirit of doubt and fear to make even relatively small commitments?

For all of you who did step forward with commitment to help us get the task accomplished, there does need to be a "thank you" over and above the "thank you" that was offered to one and all.

Likewise, the spirit of how this entire effort was begun was one of being of service and of ultimate financial help and recovery for all (not just to those involved in or contributors to the effort itself). I don't think we can turn our backs on that spirit and meaningfully succeed in the end. Let's not lose sight of this.

Over and above establishing a reserve for ongoing legal expenses, over and above paying out all scheduled bonuses, over and above additionally rewarding contributors, over and above distributing funds to all pre-registered depositors, I think we would be foolish NOT to consider the following:

a. Additional "out of court" recovery efforts—and contributing a portion of those expenses.

b. An additional contingency reserve for unforeseen expenses that might arise.

"Winning" the first battle to fully engage a specialist firm to make some sort of financial recovery is not the triumph of total victory. We can pause for brief celebration, but let us keep a view toward the battles still ahead and a commitment to our total victory.

These are my thoughts today as I tell you we are have come to the end of our fundraising efforts. For any who have been "sitting on the fence" considering whether to contribute—WOOPS!! You are welcome to remain as you are.

For those of you who have sent a contribution or an additional contribution and have yet to receive acknowledgment of receipt, you will be credited and acknowledged. If you do wish to register a (or an additional) contribution that you have mailed, do send an e-mail to: volunteerfinance @ yahoo. com. If you have yet to pre-register your deposit claim with our group, I would encourage you to do so. Please send an e-mail to our group's registry:

dptf_fb @ ziplip. com

If more information is needed, the Registrar will send you the list of informational items needed (we do not ask for account numbers).

A special thanks, again, to all who have contributed financially to our effort. WELL DONE!!!

Kind regards to all,
Ira M. Samuels

Quite why the "Recovery Fund" was closed is not very clear but undoubtedly some of the participants were becoming restless. And not surprisingly! Apart from the fact that "Ira M. Samuels" remained discreetly anonymous, so did the rest of "the recovery team" including the bankers, accountants and, most importantly, the legal team who were deputed to recover the irrecoverable.

One depositor who had contributed to the fund was confused and asked the following:

Ira, I am a little confused. Where did the 2-12 million dollars come from, and are we going after Price Waterhouse Coopers next with legal action? Will any of the 2-12 million be used to make depositors whole? If not when could they hope to see their money?

Also, where is Van with his restoration project that we have been hearing about for over 2 years?

Rick

Hello Rick,

1. *Where did the 2-12 million come from?*

    Answer: I'm not sure. The asset recovery firm we hired has simply indicated that based on their investigations, this is the initial range of funds they believe they can obtain.

2. *Are we going after PriceWaterhouseCoopers next with legal action?*

    Answer: As the world's largest public accounting firm PWC has a large legal team assembled to come to its aid in any suit that might be filed against it. Therefore, if depositors are to sue and name PWC as defendant, then the depositors need to be able to finance a team equally as large and resourceful as is PWC's. It took us over a year to raise even a token amount, hence we engaged an asset recovery team to go get us some money. I believe PWC/Wide does need to be taken to task over what happened to all of the bank's assets.

3.   *Will any of the 2-12 million be used to make depositors whole?*

     Answer: We will have to wait and see how much is recovered and how much is left after making arrangements for adequate legal counsel. Then, depending upon that answer, this question would be addressed and answered.

4.   *If not, when could depositors hope to see their money?*

     Answer: According to the Liquidator's reports that PWC has published on the PWCGlobal website, principal deposits (not counting accrued, unpaid interest) in the FIBG system were approximately $125 million. Two to twelve million dollars isn't $125 million. The hope of depositors seeing their money again rests outside of this initial recovery effort—although depending upon the results of the effort, some token payments could be made to depositors who have pre-registered with our group.

5.   *Where is Van and his restoration project that we have been hearing about for over two years?*

     Answer: He won't release any specific information, although I have seen documentation attesting to the fact that he has assembled several billion in non-liquid assets he hopes to be able to put to work to see depositors restored in full with all interest accruals.

Kind regards,

Ira

How the host of a bulletin board, allegedly also a depositor with FIBG and dedicated to retrieving the funds "mis-placed" by that bank, came to be privy to information relating to Van Brink's "several billion in non-liquid assets" is an interesting question but one that Mr. Samuels is unlikely to answer given his desire for anonymity in the past and the paucity of information he is prepared to divulge concerning his efforts. It would seem that, having milked the defrauded depositors for additional funds in the guise of a recovery fund, he felt that it was time to pack up the circus tent and roll out of town before the sheriff arrived.

That the assets of First Bank were bogus from the very beginning is incontestable and it seems probable that the alleged deposits reported were inflated by the simple process of listing fictitious amounts and crediting them, on paper, to clients, a simple creative accounting exercise with no penalty involved when there is no intention of honouring the debt in the first place. Such a manoeuvre would make the task of recovering anything from the debacle even more impossible since much of the listed deposit base would never have existed in the first place.

Van Brink remains cosily hidden away in Uganda, still protesting his innocence at great length via the Internet and no doubt enjoying the spoils of the "Asset Recovery" programme of the mysterious Mr. Samuels, whoever he may be. In view of his repeated claim that he "didn't steal the money," one wonders why (and how) he is assembling the "several billion in non-liquid assets" to re-pay clients of a bank in which he allegedly has had no involvement since his resignation in October 1999.

Which all goes to prove that P.T.Barnum was wrong—there is more than one born every minute. And Hitler was right—the bigger the fib, the more people will believe it.

"A bad man is worse when he pretends to be a saint."

—Francis Bacon

24

So Where did the Money Go?

Regardless of any so-called recovery schemes and allegations of mismanagement or downright misappropriation of funds by government or auditors, the fact is that, at the end of the day, The First International Bank of Grenada was completely and utterly bankrupt. In fact, the bank had never been technically solvent in the first place; the $100,000 in cash that it had deposited as part of its capital must have severely strained the wallets of both Brink and his Nauru based Fidelity Bank. All other monies that accrued, when deposits began to be accepted, were solely the assets and property of the clients and, as First Bank made no attempt to invest these in any legitimate form of financial vehicle to earn interest, the bank had no income of its own throughout its existence and operated solely on the incoming deposits from clients.

The unattainable rates of interest promised to depositors could only have been achieved by payouts from fresh deposits, the characteristic of every Ponzi scheme. Thus it may safely be concluded that the bank was a total sham from start to finish—and every member of the management and board of directors must have been fully aware of this and were thus equally culpable.

To be granted a banking licence in almost any jurisdiction, and Grenada was no exception, the applicants must prove that they have adequate financial resources available to guard against any possible financial malfeasance on their part, in this case $2.2 million, and that a member of the board should have had adequate banking experience. The Grenadian authorities cavalierly ignored both of these requirements in the case of First Bank and that of its many sub-banks. Not only were there never any funds available to fulfil the capital requirements but no attempt was made to verify the outlandish claims of the paper assets presented. As far as can be ascertained, no director of any bank under the First Bank's umbrella had even the slightest smattering of professional banking experience or even know-how. Van Brink's experience with Hometown Mortgage and Fidelity Bank would hardly have qualified him.

It is an old joke in accountancy that, on being asked to prepare an audit, the accountant replies, "Well yes, but what answer will you be requiring?" In the case of First Bank and Price Waterhouse, there was no doubt as to the answer that would be forthcoming—with no money in the safe, with dubious and skimpy records at best and a board of directors who refused to attend to explain themselves, there was little that liquidator Marcus Wide could do to console the depositors.

Just how much money was missing will probably never be known. Although the bank had a computer system of sorts, which Van Brink maintained he had designed in spite of his self-proclaimed lack of computer expertise, it was incapable of producing an audit trail, either by default or by design, and the unprofessional banking practices in place only added to the confusion. Significantly, in the bank's brief existence, it had proved impossible to find any accountant prepared to sign off on the accounts other than to complete a review that was based upon "facts" supplied by the bank itself and not due to any forensic investigation.

There is evidence that deposits were deliberately inflated to give a misleading impression of the bank's success. No doubt there was never any intention that the lucky one's, whose accounts were thus inflated, would ever receive the additional amounts credited but it would help to explain the staggering growth of the bank. When the end came, however, it would also mean that the auditors were chasing phantom funds that had never existed. Compounding the problem is the incontrovertible fact that many cheques never made it as far as First Bank but were neatly diverted directly to accounts in Uganda and possibly elsewhere. Thus, even an account of the monies depositors claimed to have placed with the bank are almost certainly inaccurate. This factor alone makes the "recovery fund" concept impracticable—it is, after all, not possible to recover anything that has long gone and was probably never there in the first place. The unrevealed identity of Ira Samuels, along with the bank where the funds are deposited and the identity of the "recovery agents" can only be viewed with grave suspicion, more especially since it must be more than apparent that there is nothing to recover. The contributors to this fund are those who followed the piper's tune of Van Brink and Co., believing in the unbelievable.

The British author G. K. Chesterton once said that, personally, he believed in fairies, since in order not to believe he would have had to see that they didn't exist. Perhaps it was something of this order of thinking that persuaded so many people to hitch themselves to the Van Brink wagon train—apparently unaware that it was about to go over a cliff.

Of Van Brink himself it must be said that he had, and still has, an imaginative streak in him that, had it been harnessed to more useful ends, could have taken him far—much further than a hideout in Uganda. Of his energy and ability to work there is no question, just a brief look at the outpouring of E-Mails from him in recent years can convince one of that and many a company would have been grateful of an executive with such dedication.

His personal charm and generosity are also widely acknowledged, although it has to be admitted that it is not too difficult to be generous with other people's money, but there was an undoubtedly kind and sympathetic streak in his nature.

Perhaps it is something to his credit that he is still protesting his innocence and, more remarkably, claiming that he has a plan to repay investors, surely a tacit admission that First Bank was a fraud. However, his ripostes to the findings of the auditors and the responses to questions from former clients of the bank are fatuous and self-serving, as well as being of incredible length and full of minutiae. None, however, explain satisfactorily the one major outstanding question; if The First Bank of Grenada held so many billions of dollars in assets, why were none liquidated to solve the temporary "liquidity problem?" The answer is, of course, because the assets were fraudulent and non-existent in the first place.

Van Brink was a con man who, ultimately, failed as do most of his ilk in the long run. The tragedy is that he ruined so many people's lives along the way. His repeated attempts to absolve himself from the disaster that was First Bank, and to justify his "vision," indicates that, in the end, he has he has become a victim of his own vivid imagination and has escaped from reality. Whether he will be as successful at escaping justice is another matter.

From start to finish, Van Arthur Brink was just One Big Fib.

Finis.

The greed of gain has no time or limit to its capaciousness. Its one object is to produce and consume. It has pity neither for beautiful nature nor for living human beings. It is ruthlessly ready without a moment's hesitation to crush beauty and life

—Rabindranath Tagore

APPENDIX A

The Downes Recovery Plan

Specific Efforts at Resolving the Bank's Liquidity Crisis:

A.   *As relates to the deposit protection mechanism of International Deposit Indemnity Corporation (IDIC):*

First Bank has proposed for the acceptance by IDIC of US $4.2 billion via a bearer certificate to gold deposited at UBS (Switzerland). The bearer certificate is held in safekeeping at a California securities corporation, the safekeeping receipt being in First Bank's name.

As relates to depositors being able to achieve settlement through IDIC on this basis:

1.   *A sale of the asset is in the process of negotiation by parties acting at the request of First Bank. If concluded successfully, sufficient liquidity could be available within the next 1-4 weeks for the payment of all claims against First Bank or its client banks*

2.   *Meanwhile First Bank will advance to IDIC necessary audit expenses, so that IDIC may show all potential depositor claims as contingent liabilities and its cash accounts and the $4.2 billion instrument (when authenticated) as its assets.*

3.   *Upon availability of acertified audit report, IDIC could achieve a credit line sufficient to liquidate any claims presented.*

The above is not contingent on First Bank remaining in business.

B.   *As relates to direct funding for First Bank projects: As some of you may have heard First Bank entered into a negotiation with a major world financial group for the funding of some US $21 billion in First Bank projects.*

Among those projects is the project of First Bank itself, broken down in two parts:

1.   *US $60 million to be used in clearing all outstanding demands and restoring cash reserves in excess of 10% of the bank's deposits.*

2.   *US $150 million to be used to pay a "trigger" releasing nearly US $50 billion in cash-equivalent instruments to First Bank's use.*

This assumes First Bank is still in a legal position to draw down the funding in late July/early August and to proceed as outlined.

C.   *As relates to an initial sale of Preferred Shares on 18 June 2000:*

First Bank bargained to sell US $120 million in Preferred Shares in exchange for US $120 million in Certificates of Deposit issued by Bank of China.

The subject CDs are conveyed to First Bank via Deed of Assignment. First Bank can access a credit line against these CDs upon payment to Bank of China of a one (1.00%) percent confirmation fee (US $1.2 million). Upon establishment of the credit line (estimated at 80% of the collateral value, i.e. US $96 million), US $31.7 million could be taken in cash to feed First Bank's present operational expenses and demands and the balance of US $64.3 million placed in a program to self-liquidate the credit line while giving First Bank a US $19.3 million monthly income stream.

This assumes First Bank remains in a legal position to produce the "trigger", to establish a credit line and to proceed as outlined.

D.   *As relates to re-opening of the bank's doors to deposit inflows:*

Accumulating the necessary Bank of China confirmation fee "trigger" noted in item IV, above, one of the fastest methods would be via accepting new deposit inflows (US $1.2 million being necessary to obtain the credit line from which US $31.7 million would be immediately available for operations and US $19.3 million monthly in future returns)

First Bank has present access to other proven investment programs.

No re-opening of the bank's doors to deposit inflows can occur if the bank remains under threat of a closure or a supervised liquidation action by the Government of Grenada.

E.   As relates to other income/liquidity producing efforts related to First Bank:

1. *One of the bank's holding companies is finalizing a credit line negotiation with a major financial institution in which US $53 million in financial instruments will be used to secure a credit line following the scenario outlined in item IV, above. The roll out would be approximately US $10 million monthly. Negotiations are presently set for finalization within two weeks.*

2. *The same holding company is in a separate negotiation with another bank concerning US $250 million in financial instruments and producing a net future return of approximately US $39.6 million monthly.*

3. *The same holding company is negotiating the re-sale of some of its financial instruments for immediate cash to put forward to First Bank.*

4. *The same holding company has nine other negotiations underway on various projects, each of which would produce a financial return to First Bank within 30-90 days.*

(These were the negotiations supposedly being conducted by Bob Skirving with the assistance of Van Brink in London during July/August 2000. Skirving and Brink were still in London when the Government of Grenada seized FIBG on August 11, 2000. They claimed they had successfully negotiated the placement of US $855 million in insured assets that FIBG owned to establish a line of credit from which the bank would have gained sufficient liquidity to bring all depositor obligations current. The Government of Grenada's appointed administrator of FIBG, Mr. Garvey Louison, and his successor, Erroll Thomas, wisely declined to accept their word that such a deal really existed, knowing the true status of the bank's alleged assets and bearing in mind the principal's difficulties with the truth in the past.)

5. *First Bank has several other holding companies, each of which has one or more negotiations in progress.*
    Success in any of these negotiations assumes that First Bank stays clear of a liquidation/receivership scenario, as such would either terminate the specific negotiations or suspend all such activities to produce liquidity until the liquidator/ receiver could conduct a full inventory of holdings and formulate a new plan of action.

III. The bank's options.

All of the above acts are in keeping with the spirit of the vision. But we are still left with the practical problem of how to meet the current demands.

Here, then, is what we see as the present options the bank and you have:

Option 1: Close the bank and request that IDIC step in and liquidate everything, paying all claims of all principal and interest to everyone.

In conferring with IDIC's legal counsel they estimate that such a process could take from four months to a year. The reality is that it would successfully be done and every depositor would receive every dollar deposited plus all interest owed to the date of final settlement. It would also put close to 100 Grenadians out of work and add the financial stress of their families on top of the financial stress being endured by the families of all of the bank's depositors. No one likes to think in these terms. Everyone wants to see a better solution.

Option 2: Leave the Government of Grenada on its present course and with no alternative but to close and liquidate the bank.

We view this as being less desirable than having IDIC step in and liquidate. But the Government granted the license; it has the legal right to revoke the license and to liquidate the bank.

With either Option 1 or Option 2, First Bank has to do nothing further but allow the hours and days to take their course. Both IDIC and the Government of Grenada are extremely uncomfortable, are tired of hearing excuses or promises that are never fulfilled. The daily phone traffic from depositors to both the Government and to IDIC has them to the point of no return. Yet we hope (for everyone's sake) that you, our depositors, will step in as our partners in pleading for a little more time for First Bank to set things right. Which leads me to Options 3 and 4.

Option 3: Reorganize the bank. The bank was founded in October 1997. Its original ownership has never been altered, although there have been many offers to purchase it outright. The offers were rejected because Van and the ownership believed "the vision" was more important than receiving a good selling price.

Option 4: Find a suitable buyer for the bank, one with the necessary cash to inject quickly so that everyone's life can get back to normal.

IV. The way we'd like to go.

First Bank has been experiencing a financial crisis caused by many factors (some outside of anyone's control.)

I am reminded that the Chinese written language uses various brush strokes—each stroke representing a different concept and the way those brush strokes are put together *forming other more complex concepts. The way the English word "crisis" is represented is by combining the brush strokes that represent "danger" with the brush strokes that represent "opportunity".*

And so the bank has been experiencing a crisis. My challenge is to recognize and express the opportunity that exists in the midst of the danger, to point this out and (if possible) to lead the way out of the danger by way of recognizing and moving toward the opportunity that is also present.

We've decided to pursue Options 3 and 4 simultaneously. Now, let's look for how it can be shaped in the best interests of all.

Restructuring the Bank: The Board of Directors, upon consent of the bank's ownership, has decided to put the following offer option forward for consideration by the Qualified Depositors of First International Bank of Grenada—that of becoming part of the ownership of the bank, with the option to sell the subject shares back to the bank as quickly as the bank achieves liquidity on some of its major assets.

True Value of First Bank: Undetermined. An audit is in progress.

Value Reserved for Present Ownership: To be based on final audit report, less the amount of equity subscribed to by qualified depositors, as detailed below.

Shares Offered: According to formula below:

Redemption Feature: Stock may be redeemed for cash disbursement upon liquidity being achieved by the bank, either through an acquisition by another financial entity or through its present business efforts to liquidate or borrow against present assets.

Seats on the Board of Directors: Among those qualified depositors that subscribe to stock an election will be held to give the depositors up to two nominee directors to be appointed to the board (upon the approval of the Government of Grenada). This will give the qualified depositors equal representation with the present ownership, there being an additional director, the Chairman of the Board, who presides over meetings.

The purpose of this representation is to assure qualified depositors that their investments in the bank are being well managed and that their stock may be redeemed for cash at the earliest opportunity.

The Share Acquisition Formula:

1. *Since First Bank has an immediate cash crisis (where demands for deposit withdrawals exceed the cash supply available), the highest amount of equity offered will be according to the value offset against the present demands (those on record as of June 15, 2000.)*

    The formula of exchange will be: $5.00 in redeemable stock for each $1.00 in withdrawal demands that a qualified depositor wishes to recast as a stock purchase.

No amount of present demands is required to be recast as a stock purchase order. We leave this decision entirely in each qualified depositor's hands. You may convert any portion of present demands to stock purchase or all of it to stock purchase—or leave none of your present demands altered at all.

2. *Since much of the current demands are a result of Certificates of Deposit that are set to pay the depositors monthly, the next area to look at is reducing the monthly cash demand.*

    The formula for exchange will be: $3.00 in redeemable stock for each $1.00 in a Certificate of Deposit that is recast as a stock purchase.

    No amount of your Certificates of Deposit is required to be recast as a stock purchase order. We leave this decision entirely in each qualified depositor's hands.

    You may convert any portion of your present CDs to stock purchase or all of that value to stock purchase—or leave none of your CDs altered at all.

    If you choose to re-write a portion of your CDs as stock, the remaining portion will be re-written as a CD under the original terms of that CD or those CDs.

3. *Finally, we will be awarding redeemable stock without offset of any kind, but simply based on your being a depositor (whether qualified or unqualified) at First International Bank of Grenada Limited. The award value will be $1.00 in redeemable stock for each $1.00 in ANY demand account (no exchange necessary).*

    A "demand" account is a Money Market Account or a Savings Account.

The above offer will be honored through July 31st, but based on the values of your account balances and or withdrawal demands as of June 15th.

Expectations: First Bank has several current undertakings that could produce the liquidity needed this month. But I will not tell you "It will be on Tuesday or by the end of the week..." You have had quite enough of that, I'm sure. I will tell you that the solution will occur within 90 days—and if it happens in 9 hours or 9 days, the bank will be faithful to perform in all ways to you.

A prospective buyer of the bank: NO prospective buyer has come forward with a signed offer at this time.

However, three capable buyers have expressed keen interest and discussions with each are being pursued.

When an offer is made, it is still subject to the approval of the Government of Grenada; it is not an immediate event (although we know the Government is most anxious to see an agreeable solution for all).

It should be noted that all discussions with prospective buyers are being conducted with the requirement of any sale being contingent upon cashing out the redeemable stock owners of the bank first (as described above). None of the prospective buyers have rejected this requirement.

V. What would you like to do?

Sometimes in our lives we see ourselves in situations in which we feel absolutely powerless—moments in which all of our best efforts end in frustration, embarrassment, hurt and anger. And we look around for someone to blame as a villain—believing that if we've been made a victim, there must certainly be a villain who is to blame.

In the present situation I've watched many of my colleagues go through this mental and emotional process—trying their best only to end up frustrated and embarrassed. I've watched as our wholesale banking clients have gone through the same experience, knowing that those on their inside firing lines are also going through the same experience.

The result, sadly, is that people kept in such an experience tend to start turning on each other in frustration, emotionally needing to find someone else to blame for the trouble being endured.

South Africa's Nelson Mandela said the following in a speech. Some may regard my quoting this to be quite out of place in a business letter that discusses the financial circumstances of a troubled bank. Yet I have found it to be quite insightful and very moving to my spirit—and I think it does speak to the heart of our situation. Mandela said:

"Our worst fear is not that we are inadequate. Our deepest fear is that we are powerful beyond measure.

"It is our light, not our darkness that most frightens us. We ask ourselves, 'Who am I to be brilliant, gorgeous, talented and fabulous?' Actually, who are you not to be? You are a child of God; your playing small does not serve the world.

"There is nothing enlightened about shrinking so that other people won't feel insecure around you. We were born to make manifest the glory of God within us. It is not just in some of us, it is in everyone, and as we let our own light shine we unconsciously give other people permission to do the same. As we are liberated from our own fear our presence automatically liberates others."

When I read this, when I meditate on its pure essence, I know the same spirit that inspired Mandela with this insight gave Van a vision for what First Bank could be. And I know my heart still responds to that vision. I know the hearts of many of you also still respond to that vision.

And so I ask: What is it you want to do? As depositors we can keep urging the Government of Grenada to close the bank down. We can urge IDIC to preempt such an action by melting it all down and (after a frustrating waiting period) we each can go our separate ways.

We can each of us sit on our firing lines trying to make the best of our situations, feeling that someone else is to blame and experiencing frustration and anger.

Or we can see that in our common danger there is the opportunity to forgive all that we can forgive, to give as generously as we are able, to embrace one another in unity of vision and purpose and then move forward together.

Given those choices, I know what mine is—and it is to reach out and to embrace each of you with as much forgiveness and blessing as I can provide, renewing a commitment to deal candidly with all as best I am able, and offer you all of the assistance First Bank can render in helping you plan for your future as well as helping you provide for your present.

And so I'm asking you—What do you want to do? Just fill out the below quick questionnaire and fax it to the dedicated fax machine at First Bank (By this time, the number had been disconnected by the phone company for non-payment).

Thank you for your patience. I truly apologize on behalf of First Bank (and myself) for the frustration you have experienced over the money matters in which we are responsible.

Sincerely,
Richard Downes
Chairman of the Board

Appendix B

The Jeddeloh and Hashimoto Letters

Crown Meridian Bank letter from Bruce Jeddeloh
September 21, 2000.

Dear Depositor,

I am writing this letter to explain the circumstances and truth surrounding your questions regarding the status of Crown Meridian Bank (CMB). As you are no doubt aware, CMB has, over the last few months, struggled and in many cases failed to meet its obligations to you as a direct result of CMB's relationship with First International Bank of Grenada (FIBG).

THE PAST FEW MONTHS:

As you are also no doubt aware, FIBG and its directors, officers, employees and consultants regularly gave us assurances that "everything would work out in the end." These statements, when coupled with the positions taken by the Grenadian government and IDIC, both of whom believed at the time to be independent of FIBG, continued to reinforce our belief in what they were all telling us, namely that the liquidity problems would be resolved, that payments would resume, and that this period would be remembered as a temporary inconvenience and nothing more. Delays were blamed on problems inherent with the wiring of funds, labor issues in neighboring jurisdictions, and the fact that FIBG staff was simply overwhelmed by the sheer volume of transactions.

Finally, FIBG acknowledged that it had a problem with its liquidity (i.e.short-term access to cash) but that its long-term position was excellent, given that it had an asset base of many billions of dollars and depositor liabilities of only a few hundred million dollars. This position was reinforced by IDIC's continued assurances that

FIBG had sufficient assets to meet all its obligations and by the acquiescence of Government. To date, IDIC still takes the position that FIBG will fix its "liquidity" problems and that everyone will be paid in the end.

Government was regularly made aware of our concerns, by way of written and verbal complaints, and they always gave the impression that they were acting vigilantly in enforcing the stringent provisions of the Offshore Banking Act.

For example, CMB took comfort in the fact that the Offshore Banking Act required FIBG to provide the Registrar of Companies with a statement of assets and liabilities at the close of the last business day of each quarter within thirty (30) days of the end of each quarter. The Act also required FIBG to appoint an approved auditor to prepare a report on its annual balance sheet and accounts. The Act gave the Government stringent powers to police the conduct and operations of FIBG and make any problems known to the public.

They never gave any indication to the contrary. After many months of vocalizing our complaints, while FIBG continued to give assurances, an audit was promised. After much delay, FIBG announced that the audit was completed.

However, the results were never made public. Since its alleged completion, questions have arisen as to whether or not the auditor was qualified to render an opinion, even though Government approved the auditor.

I have recently reviewed a series of documents posted on the internet at www.off-shorebusiness.com which demonstrate without doubt that the Government was aware of potentially questionable financial activity as early as summer, 1999. Although it is always easy to speak in retrospect, I am sure that we can all now question why a thorough investigation into FIBG's affairs was not made at the time of those allegations.

THE CURRENT SITUATION:

The Grenadian Government has recently appointed Mr. Garvey Louison to take control of FIBG and in doing so has given the green light to bad faith and Gestapo tactics. Mr. Louison does not appear to have the requisite experience or sophistication to conduct an international investigation of this magnitude and I fear he is out of his depth. He has apparently chosen Mr. Nabil Kassis to assist him in the investigation notwithstanding the fact that Mr. Kassis has a controversial past. (Kassis had been the manager of a hotel in Grenada, The Renaissance, and had been recruited by Van Brink earlier) *Also, strangely enough, he and the Minister of Finance seem to be relying heavily on the advice of Lawrence Jones notwithstanding the latter's involvement with recent events at FIBG.*

After being fired by the managing shareholder of ARDA, GRS & OEI for non-performance, Mr. Kassis went on to become FIBG's Chief Operations Officer, where as early as May 2000 he made many representations that normal cash flow would resume within a couple of weeks.

Based on all the false representations that Mr. Kassis has made, it is a mystery to me how Mr. Louison can be using him as his second in command, although I now understand this may no longer be the case.

On Mr. Kassis' word, vehicles owned by entities unrelated to FIBG were seized and sold, forcing the true owners to bring the matter to Court at their own cost for a final determination of ownership. No independent investigation with the Registry or any other licensing agency was conducted prior to the seizure of these vehicles. Mr. Louison simply took what Mr.Kassis had to say at face value. The registered owners of the vehicles seized by Mr. Louison have obtained injunctions against Mr. Louison and persons to whom he had hastily sold vehicles at a "knocked down" price.

Injunctions have also been obtained to prevent the sale of equipment jointly owned by affiliates of FIBG with partners in a Joint Venture Agreement.

The owners of the vehicles are also claiming from FIBG moneys held in accounts under a joint venture arrangement. A motion under the Constitution ofGrenada has been filed against Louison and the Government for the unlawful seizure of property. The court has given a conservatory order against Louison and the Government preventing them from interfering with the property. This matter will be heard on Thursday 9th October 2000 and will point the direction for other claimers against FIBG.

It is obvious that Mr. Louison's appointment of Mr. Kassis does not have an appearance of impartiality, and that it would undermine the value of any investigation if there were fraud committed by FIBG officials. It should be clear that at this point I am not accusing anyone of fraud. What I am stating is that fraud cannot be ruled out at this stage and it would therefore make sense to not have anyone whom would have had an opportunity to be involved in such fraud as a part of the investigative team.

Therefore, the appointment of Mr. Kassis shows extremely poor judgment on the part of Mr. Louison and brings his motives into serious question. The judgment and/ or motives of the Grenadian Government must be similarly questioned.

Based on the Government's inaction over the last two years and their current choice of Mr. Louison's appointment to take charge of FIBG's affairs, it is abundantly clear to me that we can not rely on them to resolve this matter for us. We need an independent third party to dissect every transaction over the last few years and to look into the personal finances of all parties involved with the operation of FIBG. These independent parties must also assess whether or not there was fraud, and if so, by whom. At this point it is unclear what will be uncovered but it is not beyond the realm of possibility that there is a conspiracy at play.

Such a conspiracy can only be uncovered if fully independent parties are involved in the investigation and prosecution of all matters.

We must take charge of our own destiny and what follows is CMB's plan for doing just that, to protect the interests of our stakeholders.

WHAT WE ARE DOING ABOUT IT:

Despite all the allegations made by FIBG detractors and all the claims made by FIBG supporters (Van Brink is purported to have written an e-mail in August and September, 2000 stating that FIBG still had billions of dollars) to date, we have still not received proper documentary confirmation from any source of whether or not FIBG has any assets whatsoever.

To this end, CMB has, in conjunction with other banks, retained the services of two highly qualified organizations. First, the law firm of Henry Hudson-Phillips (and in particular, senior counsel Mr. Karl Hudson-Phillips, Q.C.) has been retained to commence proceedings to safeguard the interest of CMB, its depositors and all those who have made investments in FIBG through CMB. Mr. Hudson-Phillips is a highly experienced and well-respected attorney and is one of the premier lawyers in the Caribbean. He is a former Attorney General of Trinidad and Tobago and has been involved in major litigation in the Caribbean over the last thirty (30) years. He also practices before the Judicial Committee of the Privy Council in London. We contacted Henry Hudson-Phillips during the first week of July 2000, after the promised audit was not delivered on time, and we have been working extensively to amass sufficient information and documentation to proceed with this action.

Mr. Hudson-Phillips and Mr. Neil Noel of the firm of Henry Hudson-Phillips & Co. held a meeting with the Minister of Finance, Mr. Anthony Boatswain and his Permanent Secretary on September 6th 2000. The Minister was advised of the concerns of CMB and its depositors in the light of the powers and duties which the Government of Grenada has under of the Offshore Banking Act.

The view was expressed to the Minister that there was need for the immediate appointment of a high profile international forensic accountant in order to investigate the affairs of FIBG since there appears to be no one in Grenada qualified to carry out this task. Mr. Hudson-Phillips suggested the name of Mr. Bob Lindquist, FCA, CFE. Mr. Lindquist comes with an impressive record of case experience from 1972 to date. He was one of the lead partners retained by the Volcker Commission to investigate dormant bank account and other assets deposited into the Swiss Bank Corporation by the victims of Nazi persecution. He has worked with Touche Ross & Co (Canada), KPMG Canada and the founder of Lindquist Avery McDonald Beskerville. He joined Price Waterhouse as a Principal in June 1996 in Washington D.C. He is now

President of Lindquist Forensics and Partners Inc. with offices in New York, Washington D.C. and Toronto.

WHY WE ARE DOING:

Should the Government of Grenada not agree to appoint Mr. Bob Lindquist or some other such experienced expert, it may be necessary for us to do so ourselves. The reason is simple. Like you, we have been hearing excuses for too long and we are no longer sure what to believe. Also like you, we have placed a lot of money with FIBG and we want it back. We are no longer comfortable waiting for IDIC or the Government to help and we are concerned that as more time passes, there is a greater risk that any assets, which may exist, are in jeopardy of being depleted. Accordingly, our goal is to move swiftly and decisively and to ensure that any remaining assets are properly distributed to the parties entitled to them, namely the depositors.

Our attorneys do not wish to jeopardize any possibility of full recovery of our moneys without litigation. However, should this become necessary we will have to do so vigorously. It may be necessary to obtain judgments in Grenada and enforce them in Grenada or any part of the world where assets of FIBG can be found.

If you feel inclined to contribute to this cause, deal directly with the lawyers for this purpose. Their wire co-ordinates will be available on the new CMB web site, discussed in greater detail below. We need an objective assessment of what went on in the background at FIBG and I believe that this is the only way to do it properly, objectively and conclusively. It is quite apparent that no one from IDIC or First Bank is willing to do that.

I have also been working on setting up an information web site for depositors at, www.crown-meridian.com, to provide you with copies of many documents involving FIBG as well as a communication channel. We can no longer afford to keep the doors open in Grenada and we have had absolutely no encouragement from First Bank to do so, but we truly want to stay in touch with everyone. With this web site, CMB will ensure that you are kept up to date with what is going on and that you are apprised as soon as something happens.

Sincerely,
By and through it's director,
Bruce Jeddeloh.
Crown Meridian Bank.

From Danny Hashimoto, Crown Meridian's other director:

As many of you know, we are busy fine tuning our records and preparing logistically for "the event"—also known as liquidity and cash payments to depositors. Although there have been some recent delays (you've read about them on IDIC's website), all of the parties involved in bringing liquidity to First Bank and we clients banks/depositors are confident that it will come.

Again, there are several parties, if you will, that are responsible for bringing this about. There is Van Brink, Richard Downes and Bob Skirving whom many of you know as the original Directors of First Bank. Now, there is the government and its appointed administrator, Garvey Louison. Granted, this administrator has walked in cold to a difficult situation and thus far has proven to be "rough around the edges." Nonetheless, he has the power to liquidate assets held by First Bank and aid in the process. Thirdly, there are top consultants to First Bank that have been diligently working toward this end as well. In the near future, I expect to hear details from any of these three parties as to liquidity and its "arrival"—the extent of coverage, etc. Also, IDIC would be quick to post a breakthrough of any sort.

IDIC, according to its September 11th website posting, is looking forward to announcing liquidity on behalf of the banks by October 11th, that is, they expect to be able to announce the processing of claims and/or serve as a disbursement conduit for the bank if necessary. What I am saying is that there are possibilities (plural) and hopefully the time element is "sooner" rather than "later"!!

Please do not pay any attention to rumors that First Bank is closed and is in full liquidation and all of its assets have been frozen (etc.). Remember this kind of rumor has been prevalent for many months now. Also, please be advised that Crown Meridian Bank is NOT closed or about to be closed. Our phone numbers remain active, Janet Carter, General Manager, and I are available at our respective business numbers—but we have pared down the overhead, until such time liquidity is realized. This is prudent as we are in the same boat as all of our depositors.

Also, there is talk of a lawsuit against First Bank by Bruce Jeddeloh on behalf of Crown Meridian Bank and some of its depositors.

Bruce has contacted a number of Crown's depositors (not all) and is asking for money to be contributed to a law firm which litigation he estimates will cost a minimum of $100,000.00. I am against this approach at this time for several reasons. Under the present status of First Bank, i.e., government appointed administrator under the Offshore Banking Act, Part IV, Sec. 20 (1)(v), it appears Court cases filed with the court could be stayed by the judge. Further, even if a case did proceed, it is unlikely that a judgement can be enforced (e.g., collection, etc.) against the bank. Sec-

ondly, I believe that the parties are close to achieving resolution, therefore, attempted lawsuits could become moot, and depositors' funds given to a law firm would literally be "retained," i.e., lost. Haven't our depositors already suffered enough financially up to this point?

Bruce Jeddeloh also talks of appointing an outside expert, a forensic accountant to come in and examine First Bank, even if the government of Grenada does not agree to the appointment. I am baffled as to how this can even be carried out as the government holds the key to the front door (and all financial records) of the bank. Sure, an investigation can be carried out on the periphery, but again it would be monies wasted, in my opinion.

In any case, know that Bruce Jeddeloh can pursue his own avenues on this matter, but he certainly does not have my approval or agreement on behalf of Crown Meridian Bank. (It is not unusual for partners to disagree at times.)

I will acknowledge that these are critical times indeed and we must all strive to make the best and soundest decisions for all concerned.

I was among the first to establish roots here and I remain committed to being here in Grenada, and especially to you, all of Crown's depositors. There is much work to be done in the weeks to come and I look forward to assisting you with your banking needs and continuing the relationships we have established which I treasure highly.

In my next update, I will provide further information regarding the website and Crown's online banking service—which will continue of course.

Thank you for your patience, understanding and perseverance.

Sincerely,
Danny Hashimoto,
Director
Crown Meridian Bank

APPENDIX C

The Plan

Some Key Elements in the Economic Plan for Participation in the African Union Reserve System

By
Van A. Brink

Introduction: The Keys to Development

The "ABC" formula for governmental self-sufficiency: The governments of Alaska (a state in the USA) and certain oil-rich nations have a common problem each year. Their problem is that governmental incomes far exceed the expenses incurred in providing all essential services to their peoples, including cradle-to-grave health care services, schools and colleges, police protection, fire protection, roads and maintenance, etc. And so each year those government's leaders are faced with the task of determining not only the budgets of government services to be curtailed, maintained or expanded, but also how much of the revenue surplus to simply give away to each of their citizens.

This mutual problem arose, of course, because each government properly identified the valuable natural resources of its jurisdiction. But more than mere identification, these governments:

(A) Understood that governments seldom make sound business operating decisions—that the politics of decision making and managerial appointments by government all but guarantees bloated bureaucratic chaos, corruption and fiscal meltdowns;

(B) Allowed non-political, private interests to profitably develop the jurisdiction's resources only under development, export and royalty agreements with the government;

(C) The result being that those who are properly motivated to manage costs and still achieve a profit can simply factor into their business planning the philosophical, environmental, legal and financial needs/requirements of government.

The result of this simplistic "ABC" formula for economic development is that the development, export and royalty agreements implemented now produce so much revenue that these governments have no need to tax their citizens at all. Moreover, there is an overflowing of revenue to the point where excess cash is given away each year to citizens.

The overall plan proposed by the African Union Reserve System ("AURS") entails more than establishing an improved central banking authority in the participating nation and a new asset-backed currency, the Plan identifies key natural and political/economic resources of of a nation and seeks to utilize these in such a way as to promote the economic health and vitality of the nation, establishing its government as wholly self-sufficient (independent of the need to rely upon tax revenues on the incomes of businesses and individuals).

Why the emphasis on governmental independence from income taxation? The plain truth is that no presently developed nation on earth achieved its own fundamental development in the face of significant taxing of the incomes of its individual citizens, its businesses or its industries.

Ancient Rome, for instance, did have a system of taxation—but such taxation was imposed on the foreign lands they conquered (on the subjects of Rome), not on the citizens of Rome.

The amazing industrialization of America during the 19th and early 20th centuries occurred in an income tax-free environment. When the income tax was instituted in the early part of the 20th century, it was done so at the minuscule rate of one percent. The debate was heated in the U.S. Congress about imposing an absolute ceiling of three percent, a proposal which was finally defeated for fear it would soon encourage an increase up to that level (which was viewed as unnecessary and unacceptable). America's industrialization continued at a breath-taking pace.

Europe during the industrialization era also enjoyed an income tax-free (or nearly free) environment, relying on the support and natural wealth of its colonial empires to fuel the home treasuries (and factories). It was only AFTER the foundation of internationally competitive industrialization was firmly established that any of the presently economically powerful nations moved toward significantly taxing the incomes of individuals, businesses and industries.

Yes, we can look at post-World War II Japan, western Germany and Europe and see fantastic development with simultaneous income tax expectations by those governments. But consider the massive outside aid programs that were the foundation of such redevelopment. Their reemergence was not achieved by the struggling (and ravaged) nations' own independent means.

Each of the other elements of the overall AURS Plan can be linked similarly to fundamental economic principles which we will not even discuss here in brief. Most of these principles are already commonly understood or rely on The "ABC" formula for governmental self-sufficiency. Let's move on, then, with outlining "the Plan."

I.
Overview of the Plan

A. The Beneficial Objectives for a Participating Nation:

A wise man once commented that it is difficult to remember that your original objective was to drain the swamp when you find yourself up to your waist in alligators. At the outset, then, let us clearly state the objectives of the Reserve so that they may guide us in our ventures into the economic swamp:

(1) To provide or to facilitate the development of necessary infrastructure and services (roads, schools, hospitals and other essential governmental services) and to enable the economic development and prosperity of the nation's people without the government resorting to taxes of any kind upon the people, businesses and industry; and

(2) To provide for the present control and the orderly removal from circulation of the fiat currency presently printed by participating nation's central bank (which has foreign exchange value limitations in neighboring countries—and little to no recognition or exchange value in many international markets) and to institute a stable, asset-backed currency, utilizing the nation's natural resource potentials without eliminating in the process the immediate-and long-term private profit incentives of the nation's people.

(3) To initiate controls on the development of natural resources, said controls to encourage environmentally sound development of the resources, render a favorable system of compensating those who develop the natural resources, and to ensure the financial self-sufficiency of each participating nation's Government and the long-term viability and expansion of an asset-backed currency in national and international commerce.

(4) To situate participating nations as world centers for business, industry and finance.

(5) To elevate the participating nation as a non-belligerent leader among nations in the philosophical and political movement for the freedom of all peoples.

B. Identifying the a nation's most precious resources:

Identifying, developing and controlling a revenue stream from their distinctive precious resources is what situated the governments of Alaska and several oil-rich nations for their long-term self-sufficiency and provided for the overflowing abundance of their peoples.

What are the precious resources of your nation? We would suggest that among the resources are these:

(1) National political sovereignty and the unhindered ability to enter into treaties and agreements which enhance the present and future well being of the nation; and

(2) Certain natural resources.

(3) Agricultural export ability.

Yet in the face of these very real abilities many developing nations in Africa struggle for finances to meet the needs of the people, the national currency has only limited acceptance outside of the nation, needed expansion of infrastructure usually exists only on a low priority scale and the economic advancement of the people has been stunted.

C. The Five-Pronged Strategy for Economic Self-Sufficiency:

The African Union Reserve System proposes a plan utilizing five separate (but inter-related) strategies.

Strategy Area No. 1:

The Natural Resources Development Corporation: Providing for the development of a participating nation's natural resources in a manner consistent with the national interests, while preserving private incentives and initiative.

Initially, the focus will be on minerals production. Components to be added later will be in relation to timber and agricultural production.

Strategy Area No. 2:

The Currency Issue and Control Functions of the Reserve: Establishing an asset-backed currency, beginning with control over the existing currency, then with the systematic redemption of that fiat currency so that the national government and the people are not economically injured in the process.

Strategy Area No. 3:

The Central Banking Functions of the Reserve: Creating a strong central banking system for the participating nation, one which assures depositor safety, banking stability and profits, while encouraging expansion of banking services and structuring meaningful bank incentives to provide low interest loans in the private business and consumer sectors.

Strategy Area No. 4:

The International Business Center Corporation: Establishing the participating nation as an international business, industry, and financial services nation—as a Switzerland of Africa, so to speak.

Strategy Area No. 5:

Ministry of Diplomatic Relations: Establishing the participating nation as a world champion in the cause of freedom for all peoples, while instituting and maintaining its status as a nonbelligerent among the nations.

Utilizing the "ABC" formula for economic development, each of these key strategy components support the whole in accomplishing the objectives. What follows is a narrative explanation of each of these strategies.

II.
The African Union Reserve System

In General: The Reserve is structured to operate for the benefit of participating governments and for the protection of a small consortium of private interests that are providing the underlying financial strength and will arrange for the managerial and training expertise necessary to develop the strategies and achieve the goals outlined herein.

For its part and as consideration for the governmental cooperation necessary for the undertaking, the Reserve agrees to guarantee the reasonable national budgets of the Government for the reasonable term of the Reserve's contracted involvement. Assets initially pledged by the Reserve to this undertaking amount to the equivalent of US $10 billion.

The conditions of this financial guarantee are (1) the planned removal of income taxation by the participating nation's people and their businesses; (2) that the Reserve be left a-political in nature, obligated to perform and to cooperate as agreed with any government in power, but supporting no political parties or personalities; (3) the immediate declaration of the participating Government that it is a neutral, nonbelligerent among the nations; (4) the incorporation with the Reserve of all central banking functions and control over the existing and the new currency; and (5) the participating Government's enactment of such legislative framework as from time to time may be necessary to fully implement the strategies contained herein and any necessary adjustments or additions thereto.

A. The Reserve's Initial Organizational Structure:

(1) Board of Trustees: Chairman, Vice Chairman, Secretary, Treasurer, and the participating nation's Minister of Finance.

(2) Executive Operating Committee: Chief Executive Officer, Chief Financial Officer, Chief Operating Officer, Chief of Data Processing, and Chief of State Relations.

(3) Advisory Board: Economic Statistics, Commercial Banking, Offshore Banking, Overseas Banking, Domestic Public Relations, International Public Relations, and Deposit Insurance.

(4) Administrative Board: Comptroller of the Currency, Director of Reserve Acquisitions, Director of Central Banking Operations, Director of Investments, Director of Foreign Exchange, Director of International Banking, Director of Electronic Systems & Development, Director of Reserve Guarantees and Loan Programs, Director of Public Relations & Education, Director of Government Services, Director of Data Processing, Director of Plant Development, Director of Legislative Development, Director of Legal Affairs, Director of Corporate Interests, and Director of Security Services & Transportation.

III.
The Five Strategies

A. Strategy No. 1: Natural Resources Development Corporation:

The purpose of the corporation is to encourage the environmentally-friendly development of the participating nation's natural resources, to provide managerial oversight to such development, and to assure that the economic strength of the Reserve is enhanced (to the immediate and continued benefit of the financial stability and solvency of the Government, to the medium-and long-term national and international expansion of the currency, and to the medium-and long-term financial protection of the other beneficiaries of the Reserve).

The initial functions of the Corporation will be: (1) to absorb experienced personnel from existing governmental agencies which regulate natural resources; (2) to establish export and royalty agreements with existing business and industrial private interests; and (3) to facilitate additional natural resources development.

In all respects the goals of the Corporation are to ensure the environmentally-friendly development on the participating nation's natural resources; to create a local-friendly employment atmosphere; to develop the financial resources of the Reserve (and, hence, of the nation); and to honor the Government's existing concessions and licensing of active producers.

B. Strategy No. 2: The Currency Management Functions of the Reserve:

The Reserve must have absolute control over the nation's monetary system. This includes both the present currency and the new asset-backed currency to be instituted by the Reserve.

(1) The Present Currency: While the new currency is being developed, the existing currency of each participating nation will continue to be used.

With the changing of control over the present currency from the Government and the existing central bank to the Reserve, the Reserve may back authorized use of the present currency with financial instruments from top 100 world banks so as to engender more public and international confidence in the existing currency.

(2) The New Monetary System: Some would argue that there is no need to back a currency or a monetary system with tangible assets, since (for examples) neither the American nor the British monetary system is presently backed by precious metal. The fact remains that both the American and the British monetary systems were originally backed by precious metals—and that it was during this period in which the monetary systems of those nations were precious metals backed that those nations grew to world economic prominence,even dominance. That their fiat currencies are still accepted is based on the international recognition they have gained as industrial and consumer superpower nations (and that they can pretty much do as they please by way of military muscle).

Swiss Francs have also been internationally respected, not because of the industrial strength of the nation, not by reason of international fear over the military power of the Swiss, but because as a militarily-neutral nation of but modest industrial power, the Swiss have backed their currency with gold.

It is interesting to note that the nation with the highest per capita standard of living in the entire world is not the United States, Great Britain, Japan, Canada, Russia, Germany, France or any other large European nation. It is Switzerland. Even more than industrial or military power, national and international confidence in the monetary and banking systems of a nation provides not only the foundation for the prosperity of a nation's peoples, but the superstructure as well.

(3) The URS Monetary Symbol: In instituting the new monetary system for the participating nation the AURS will utilize URS usage of two carat (^^) symbols. The carat symbol is convenient (found on most typewriters and computer keyboards as Shift-6), and is not (to our knowledge) presently the symbol of any other nation's currency.

(4) The Value of the New Currency is to be periodically set, not floating, and based on a multi-national average of prices indices for various tangible assets according to the tangible, appraisable properties held by the AURS.

(5) Design of the New Currency: On the obverse of the note, utilize multinational, happy children playing. On the reverse side, utilize pictures of African animals. Such a theme could be carried out for both coins and paper currency (the currency should be printed by four color process). Since we are instituting one of the most valuable currencies in the world, let us also make it the most attractive currency in the world.

Possible motto: "Our future depends on all of us"

Universally, children are seen as being the future of a family and of a nation. All parents wish to see a bright future for their children.

Instituting an asset-backed currency establishes a sound financial base upon which the future may be developed.

On paper currency, signatures by a participating nation's Minister of Finance and by the the AURS Comptroller of the Currency. A color flag of the nation next to the Minister's signature. Seals screened in background for both the participating nation and the AURS. French language with English sub-titles. Sizing: English Pound note sizes, since increasing note denomination sizes allow for increasingly legible sub-titles, as well as for the ease of sorting the currency.

(6) Printing/Minting of New Currency: Considerations given most weight in deciding where to have minting/printing completed are these: (1) international secrecy, (2) absolute security and integrity of the manufacturers, and (3) proximity/logistical security. The final consideration would be as to cost economy.

(7) Protection of the Currency: Since we are undertaking to remove a baseless currency from circulation and institute a currency which is wholly asset-backed, much care needs to be taken to design a currency extremely difficult to counterfeit, to protect the means of production of the currency, the stores of currency, and the precious metals and diamond reserves and other asset-backing of the currency. To this end there needs to be a special force of highly trained, highly disciplined, well compensated police/investigative personnel who are completely trustworthy. This force, under joint control of the Government and the Reserve, must be ever vigilant in their tasks of protecting currency and asset stores, as well as efficiently and thoroughly investigating any possibility of counterfeiting, so as to protect the absolute integrity of the new economic foundation. With respect to printing, for instance, the printing plates must be kept in the Reserve's custody and security at all times and returned to the Reserve by such security personnel at the end of each run. It is also important that, if possible, the Reserve gain and

maintain custody of all printing plates for the existing currencies so as to avoid flooding the market with the baseless currency being printed for redemption/exchange to the new currency.

(8) Redemption of Existing Currency: Upon issuance of the new currency the AURS would offer a short period in which one could exchange old currency for the new currency.

In redeeming the existing currency special care is to be taken to avoid the redemption of counterfeit currency—granting amnesty to (and a reduced exchange rate to) any who come forward to make such conversions in the first 3 to 5 days and prosecuting any who would attempt to do so thereafter.

(9) Use by the Reserve of the old currency: The old currency will not be destroyed, but will be warehoused until the expiration of exchange value.

The notes will then be bundled for sale as "game money" and "poker money" to consumers worldwide. "One Hundred Thousand Francs" ($29.95) or "Be a Millionaire" (only $149.95) or "Genuine Counterfeit Francs" (only $49.95)

In the packages of game money, the AURS would insert a color brochure describing the new currency, its backing, a pictorial tour of the participating nation, the wild animals in their natural habitat, a brief history of the country, an invitation for tourism ("We'll greet you with free money samples, if you come." and "[Name of Nation]—Absolutely priceless, and worth every carat.")

The object, here, is not to make a fortune selling canceled or counterfeit currency (although the additional foreign currency proceeds could prove useful), but to expose the world to the new asset-backed currency of the participating nation. For the country to emerge as a world financial center services nation, the world must become intimately introduced to what it is that the nation has to offer.

It could be that demand for the "game money" old currency will out pace the supply of the redeemed old currency. The makers of the board game called Monopoly, for instance, print more face value in game money each day than does the Federal Reserve System. For this reason, the plates for printing the old currency should be retained in the physical possession of the Reserve (and the Reserve will ultimately need to construct its own bank-note production facility for absolute control of both the genuine new currency and the genuine old currency).

(10) International Use: Foreign and Offshore banks may electronically participate by having correspondent relations with a commercial bank in the nation or
with the Reserve's Central Banking Center directly (higher reserve requirements
apply). There is no reason why any bank anywhere in the world cannot link
directly with the Reserve and have correspondent relationships with commercial
banks in the nation—the main factor is to correlate with international exchange
rates and to be able to scan electronically to assure that the appropriate balances
are available.

Those international business and industries which locate in the new Business and
Industry Development Zones (see Strategy No. 4) and those nations receiving
diplomatic recognition from the participating nation (see Strategy No. 5) would,
by treaty, recognize and utilize the AURS Carat. It is recommended that all
nations (regional or abroad) that wish to establish diplomatic relations with the
participating nation, by treaty or agreement, cause their central banks to recognize the AURS currency.

(11) International Exchange Rates: Initially, international exchange rates would
be set, not floating (as discussed in "Value of the Currency"). Each world currency would be evaluated from time to time to establish the exchange rate.

C. Strategy No. 3: The Central Banking Functions of the Reserve:

Many functions of the existing central bank will remain in tact, although the
bank monitoring system will be brought into the electronic age with all banks
subject to full implementation of the system provided.

(1) Check Clearing Facilities: Among the first year improvements will be regional
check clearing facility for commercial banks, enabling their customers to engage
in commerce throughout the participating nations and have overnight clearing of
payments they received by check.

(2) Tools for Internal Management Monitoring: Among the features of the fully
Y2K-compliant computerized bank operating system are daily, weekly, monthly,
quarterly and annual management monitoring functions which allow a bank's
senior management to gain an up-to-the-minute overview of any component of
their banking operation or of the whole operation. In turn, this allows for readily
available information essential to central banking forecasts, as well as compliance
monitoring.

(3) Implementation of Central Bank Loan Programs for Commercial Banks: Once commercial banks are comfortable with the electronic information management system and once the new currency is implemented, the Reserve will be able to implement several new loan programs involving banks in a participant nation, including a general bank loan program at very low rates to enable greater commercial bank lending ability in the private sector, a residential mortgage program whereby long-term, low-interest loans will be made available to the consumer (while maintaining bank profitability in management the loans), agricultural development loans, commercial loans, industrial loans, mining loans, venture capital loans, and micro-lending programs.

(4) International Currency Accounts: Commercial banks may have international currency accounts to the extent that actual currency is in their possession (and reported at close of business each day) or held at a Central Banking Center. Electronic accounts in foreign currencies at foreign banks must be held with AURS oversight on the movement of funds, so as to assure that clientele of participating banks who have foreign currency accounts are able to depend that either the cash exists in the safe of the bank, at the Central Banking Center, or at a foreign bank with AURS' guarantee that such funds are freely available.

Deposit Insurance: Commercial banks may be given the option of participating in the Reserve's deposit insurance program or arranging independently for approved deposit insurance coverage. To the fullest extent possible,depositors worldwide must have good reason for complete confidence in the AURS banking system.

D. Strategy No. 4: The International Business Center Corporation:

The development of the participating nation as a premier center for business and industry is the long-term goal, the spill-over benefits being business-financed development of infrastructure and increased human resource development for the nation's people.

While the focus of this corporation is the development of "offshore sector" business and industry, the overall format could be adapted (in the future)for the expansion and development of onshore business and industry, as well.

In this respect grant monies or low-interest loans could be offered by the AURS for selected types of enterprises deemed essential to the development of the nation.

Here are the basics:

(1) By legislation create the nation's Development Corporation (a draft of this legislation is available).

(a) The Development Corporation is to be owned by AURS.

(b) The purpose of the Development Corporation is to promote the development of the nation as an appealing international business and industrial nation and in so doing to collect license fee consideration for the Government. Spill over benefits include increased national employment opportunities and infrastructure development of the country, as more than one Development Zone may be named by the Development Corporation.

(c) Legislation also declares that businesses and industries which incorporate in and locate in the Development Zone are also exempt from income taxes, import duties and export duties (unless export is to the participating nation).

(d) The Development Corporation enters into long-term contracts with private companies: (i) National Investment Corporation; and (ii) National Management Corporation. Each of these corporations will receive 25% of the license fees generated, 50% going to the Development Corporation. (Drafts of these agreements are available.)

(e) The Investment Corporation procures land for use as the Development Zone. In exchange for this it receives 25% of fee income to be generated plus 75% of lease income from the property itself.

(f) The Management Corporation does international marketing and management of the Development Zone in exchange for 25% of fee income to be generated.

(2) Property is identified, purchased by the Investment Corporation and declared to be an International Business and Industry Development Zone by the Development Corporation. With this declaration comes tax-exempt status for the property itself.

(3) Legislation is also implemented in the following areas (draft legislation is completed and would be made available after ratification of the AURS Plan and initial implementing legislation):

(a) International Business Companies Act (no business or industry may locate in the Development Zone unless it has been registered under this act).

(b) International Trusts Act.

(c) The Registered Agent and Trustee Licensing Act.

(d) International Mutual Funds Act.

(e) International Stock Exchange Act.

(f) International Banks Act.

License fees are shared according to the formula in III(D)(1) above.

Companies formed under the above Acts are income tax-exempt in the nation and are eligible for duty-free status on imports.

(Note: An explanation of and an initial legislative proposal for the establishment of the International Business Center Corporation is available. Upon establishment of this legislation, additional draft legislation for the following Acts will be made available: International Bank Act; International Trust Act; International Mutual Funds Act; The Registered Agent and Trustee Licensing Act; the International Stock Exchange Act; and the International Business Companies Act.)

E. An Ancillary Component Strategy—The World Investors' Stock Exchange:

Both onshore and offshore corporations may list their stocks for public trading. Unlike other stock exchanges, the capital of investors is guaranteed through Stock Value Guarantees issued by the Reserve.

(Note: Draft stock exchange implementing legislation is completed and will be submitted upon implementation of the International Business Companies Act.)

F. Strategy No. 5: The Nation's "World Freedom Zone":

As explained more fully in a paper titled Inverting a Developing Nation's Economic Paradigm, the long-term economic potential of diplomatic recognition as a revenue engine is significant. There are also spill-over benefits of tourism, local employment and infrastructure development.

(1) In essence a Government realizes the revenue potential of granting diplomatic recognition to existing nations, aspiring nations and governments in exile.

(2) Additional economic benefits may be gained through allowing an aspiring nation to develop a given territory over an extended period (such as the British

did for China by developing Hong Kong, then turning it back over to Chinese rule after so many years).

(3) The potential exists for the declaring of "World Freedom Zones" through creation of a World Freedom Zone structure similar to the format presented above for International Business and Industry Development.

IV.
Politics Aside

Does the AURS have economics all figured out? No. No one in the world has ever mastered economics.

Those who have tried to master it by totalitarian control and gun-point have usually stagnated or ruined their national economies (along with inflicting upon their people massive deprivation and suffering, no matter how noble their original intentions might have been).

Those who have tried to master it through taxation always seem to walk along the brink of disaster. And since taxation is also, ultimately, at gun-point and families cannot always afford the taxes imposed on them, the attempt to master economics by this method also exacts its toll in human misery.

Those who have attempted to master it through a flexible monetary policy controlling the issuance of non-asset-backed (fiat) currency have learned to tremble at the mention of the word "inflation", seeing many recent historical examples (including in the 1990s) of countries that have been absolutely ruined by runaway government money-printing machines.

There is no subtler, no surer means of overturning the existing basis of society than to debauch the currency. The process engages all the hidden forces of economic law on the side of destruction, and does it in a manner which not one man in a million can diagnose. I didn't say this. No one connected with the AURS said this. John Maynard Keynes said it (The Economic Consequences of the Peace, page 235).

One of the major problems facing developing countries is that their national currencies that have little meaning in the rest of the world. Overthrowing or democratically removing one government and installing another has been done in most, if not all developing nations. Printing a new baseless currency has been done in many developing nations. Usually, economic conditions for the peoples of those nations were not meaningfully changed by either of these approaches and not by a combination of these methods either.

The AURS proposes to go to the root of the economic woes of developing nations, to implement a currency the nation and the world can rely upon, to implement a central banking system and the nations' development of natural resources from the "ABC" method rather than from the political appointee method, and to use resulting revenues in government finance and economic development for each participant nation.

The AURS Plan is not about politics, political personalities or proving anyone to be either good or bad. The people of a developing nation can decide such matters for themselves at the ballot box come every election.

What they cannot decide for themselves is the international credibility of their paper currency. Many can't even rely on that currency at home. What they cannot do is make needed infrastructure magically appear when the equipment must be imported and the nation's currency is unacceptable to the sellers of such equipment.

So do we sit by and wonder how it will all turn out? Or do we volunteer a plan to help that can help developing nations?

Is the AURS Plan perfect? I am confident that it is not. I am confident, also, that it is a starting place, a new beginning for developing nations.

It is not the perfect end. The peoples of these nations must find such for themselves, individually and collectively. They must dream their own dreams,pursue their own aspirations, they must achieve for themselves the local,regional, national and international destinies they alone decide are worthy.

The best that anyone from the outside can do is step up and share a set of "right tools", then get out of the way and let them go to work together.

I believe the AURS Plan does this.

What the AURS will need is local administrators and staff who see the vision and who will share in it by dedicating themselves to its development and fulfillment in their nation.

While the AURS Plan entails the making and regulation of money, real money, it is not about money. It is about liberation from the perceived necessity for governmental tax oppression. And it is about empowerment of the individual, of the entrepreneur, of the inventor, of the businessman, of the industrialist, of the laborer, of the tradesman and of the farmer. These are the ones who will bring development to their nations and prosperity to themselves, their families and their communities.

The AURS is not about foreign exploitation. It is about finding an end to the necessity for submission to exploitation in international trade situations due to the lack of having a currency readily recognized at full face value by principal trading partners.

The European community has recognized the inherent weakness of their respective national currencies in international trade. Each time goods or services are procured in the international market, the local currency and economy suffers. Having a common currency for use among principal trading partners can act to relieve such routine and avoidable suffering.

Seen from the larger perspective the AURS Plan can bring about not only national blessing, but regional and continental relief from the shared misery of certain foreign trade issues, as more and more trading-partner nations see the benefits of adopting the AURS common currency.

The AURS Plan is not a "magic pill" that immediately relieves all governmental or economic problems. But it is a plan to put each participating nation on the road to economic health and vitality.

APPENDIX D

In September 2000, when First Bank's structure was collapsing around the ears of its hapless depositors, Van Brink found time to pen the following so-called "Practical Guide to Money Laundering." His motive for publishing this oddity is unknown but presumably it whiled away the time in Kampala and was an attempt to justify partially himself in the eyes of his depositors. Unfortunately, it has not been possible to corroborate the touching details relating to his college days, where, you will recall, he achieved the remarkable distinction of earning a Ph.D. in Economics at a faculty that granted no degrees.

Inadvertently, in recounting his attempt to deposit cash into a Grenada bank, he reveals his total ignorance of normal banking procedures—yet he bases this "guide" on his years of experience as a private offshore banker.

VAN BRINK'S PRACTICAL GUIDE TO MONEY LAUNDERING
by Van A. Brink (September 18, 2000)
© 2000 by Workingdraft Publishing, Ltd. All Rights Reserved.
Permission is hereby granted for distribution and/or republication in its entirety.

It is nearly impossible to read any newspaper article these days about Van Brink or First International Bank of Grenada ("First Bank") and not come up with the smell of criminal activity, such as money laundering. And since, internationally, I am now regarded as a confirmed and undisputed expert in the subject matter, I think it is time to go ahead and set out in writing a very "Practical Guide to Money Laundering." This Guide is thoughtfully based on my years of private offshore banking experience.

First of all, have I actually done it?

I'll admit when I was first asked that question (in the early days of Fidelity International Bank, First Bank's predecessor), I had to carefully think. In my mind I had only two images of "money laundering." The first image had to do with the $100 bill I had lost one week, only to find it safely inside the front pocket of my freshly laundered jeans the next. But by the intense, almost "I'm in the know and won't let on about you" tone, I sensed that the person asking me the question "Had I done it?" wasn't talking about that week's personal laundry mistake (although I've since tried to be mindful of checking my pockets first before throwing my pants in a laundry basket—in this sense, I am, indeed, an admitted money launderer).

The second mental image I had was engendered by the Tom Cruise/Gene Hackman movie, "The Firm", where a prestigious southern law firm was involved in helping a major crime family "launder" money in an offshore bank located in the beautiful Caribbean Cayman Islands. While I didn't remember the movie as portraying suit cases and airplane cargo-holds stuffed with cash, that sense was certainly there.

Interestingly enough, that same sense permeates the whole world of individuals who are convinced they can help you put together a major deal based on the billions of dollars worth of paper assets you may be holding and representing. While I spent a month in London, recently, attempting to assist the First Bank Board of Directors in negotiations regarding the bank's large assets, no sooner would people hear my name or the fact that First Bank was an offshore bank in the Caribbean, than I would be approached (or the other First Bank parties sitting with me at the table) with overt or thinly-disguised offers of direct assistance in laundering the presumed large sums of cash we must also, surely, be secretly representing. No amount of protesting that we had no cash to launder was believed. Finally, at meeting new experts, we would wait the five to ten minutes before the topic was raised, roll our eyes at each other, refuse to protest but just re-direct the topic of conversation to the matters at hand.

Have I done this "suitcase-style" of money laundering? No.

So why is it that offshore bankers are presumed to be the representatives of large sums of cash that needs to be "laundered?" After four years of offshore banking experience, I can truthfully say, "I don't have a clue."

And I'll add this: "I have yet to see one suitcase filled with money."

But having been presumed to be a money launderer, over the past four years I've managed to sneak in a few minutes of thought as to what it would actually take to effectively launder millions, tens of millions or hundreds of millions of dollars in US currency (or any other brand for that matter).

What it would take:

1. The ability to post it electronically and then transmit it electronically to the desired destinations, worldwide. Okay, who has that ability? Answer: a nation's large commercial banks.

Why do I say that? Answer: Because private offshore banks must deal with commercial banks to be connected to the electronic banking infrastructure.

So could a private offshore bank in the Caribbean (or any other area with small tax-haven jurisdictions) accept cash, take it to a commercial bank, deposit it and have it credited electronically?

It would be difficult. Let me tell you why, based on direct experience (I did, after all, promise that this would be a "Practical Guide").

Several months after we landed bank operations on Grenada (and before Mr. David Marchant ever got the nod to commence an attack on the bank's and my legitimacy), we suddenly realized one afternoon that there was not enough in the local Grenadian bank account to clear the payroll checks that were due to be released the next morning.

Being the brilliant problem-solver that I am (when I was told this by telephone), I said, "No problem, just call up St. Vincent and have them wire the $30,000 EC (equivalent to $11,100 USD) down to the Grenada account. Piece of cake!"

And to this on-command, legendary male problem-solving-ability-in-an-instant bit of condescending advice I had just offered, my female Chief Financial Officer patiently replied that she had already made the call—that the St. Vincent bank's wire service for the afternoon had already cut off.

Not willing to be shown a fool for not having a quick and ready answer upon command, I said, "Well, the bank is still open, isn't it? Have someone go down to the bank, draw out the $30,000 EC in cash, jump on the evening shuttle for the 20-minute flight and then deposit the cash in the morning.

A Grenada bank can take Eastern Caribbean Dollars on deposit, can't they?"

She then queried me, obviously seeking some of that manly, authoritarian assurance for which I am so famous: "Do you really think that best? We could just explain the situation to the employees and tell them their checks will be one day late. I mean, we've never made a cash deposit before and I'd feel a little strange walking in with $30,000 and stepping up to the teller window. You know how suspicious everyone is about offshore bankers—they'll probably think we're money laundering or something."

I tried to be kind, gentle, understanding and reassuring. Honest, I did. I didn't yell and I didn't scream; I calmly said, "Don't be silly. It's not a lot of money. I'm sure they have larger cash deposits every day from grocery stores and such. It will be fine. Let's not upset the employees and inconvenience their families. They are owed their pay; let's give it to them on time, even though it costs us a plane ticket and a night in a hotel for someone."

My Chief Financial Officer reluctantly agreed, volunteering to put the courier up at her home for the evening to save the hotel expense.

And so it was that in the morning she took the $30,000 EC cash deposit and walked into the one commercial bank in all of Grenada that would have anything to do with a sleazy offshore bank. Upon seeing the cash deposit tendered, the teller's eyes bulged and she excused herself for a moment and went to the bank's manager who came out to ask my CFO to kindly take a chair for a few minutes. The few minutes passed and a Grenadian Police Detective arrived, whereupon my CFO was grilled for nearly three hours as to the source of funds, why she would be carrying so much in cash, what the bank was really up to, why we didn't have the money wired or tell the employees to wait a day—you know, the basics a commercial bank would want to know before it became party to one of those notorious money laundering operations everyone knew private offshore banks are really all about.

Later that day I lived through the "I told you's" that other men have also been made to suffer as thanks for their fine, instant problem-solving abilities. And when (a few weeks later) a client bank director invited me to a dinner with one of that bank's prospective depositors (a married couple), I confess to rolling my eyes for the first time when someone offered a deposit. You see, they had US $5,000 in cash left over from the $10,000 they had brought with them on their trip to the Caribbean and thought it would be easier to just leave the money as a deposit, rather than take the cash back home with them, re-deposit it at their local bank, then wire the funds back to Grenada. I reluctantly agreed, when I came up with another instant-on-demand male executive problem-solving solution of issuing the Certificate of Deposit, booking it in our accounts as a liability to the bank, and then crediting it to Petty Cash and just living with it for a while. Male pride is such a wonderful thing. We can solve any problem.

Just ask one of us.

A friend recently told me that the current theory (September 2000) about why I'm trying to "help First Bank" (when I did resign and separate from the bank in October 1999) is that I'm "hanging around to stall people" while I "hide the money" and that's why I've chosen to hang out in Uganda, Africa.

This sort of theory seems to play well in the Uganda press, as well.

But pardon me if I now ROFLOL (computer speak for "Roll On the Floor while Laughing Out Loud)." Grenada's annual per capita income is approximately US $6,000; Uganda's is US $300. If (before all the adverse publicity) someone known to be associated with me is all but arrested in Grenada for daring to deposit the equivalent of US $11,100 in cash, just how on earth would I cleverly hide millions and billions in Uganda and go undetected? Please.

Okay, so back on subject—What would it take to launder large sums of money?

1. The ability to post it electronically and then transmit it to the desired destinations, worldwide, i.e. be a large commercial bank. How is only a large commercial bank able to do such?

2. By absorbing the cash in the bank's normal operations. And just what "normal banking operations" would accommodate the absorption of tens and hundreds of millions in cash?

3. Well, you could use it to stuff the automatic teller cash machines (hint: private offshore banks don't have any), or

4. You could rotate it through your vaults so that tellers in all of your branches have adequate cash supplies for daily business (hint: private offshore banks don't have tellers that have cash and make change—most private offshore banks, therefore, don't have any vault, no matter how small).

5. Is there any other way to absorb large amounts of cash in a banking operation? Sure. Have equally large amounts already in the electronic system and use the cash you receive as Petty Cash in your operations.

Problem is, I wouldn't have a clue on how to utilize $1 million or $10 million in Petty Cash each week, no matter how many two-martini lunches I authorized for all bank executives, nor would I care to warehouse all of the pencils, pens and staples that such an amount of money would buy each week.

Would you?

6. Still (as of the month I spent in London in July/August 2000), I have been told there are yet other ways for offshore bankers to launder huge amounts of cash: make the right contacts with the large commercial bankers in the United Kingdom who know how to absorb enormous amounts of cash and don't charge too much for the service. I understand the same is true in America. Woops—that was my first point: big nation, large commercial banking is the only way to do it. I've also heard that there are Arabian sultans and sheiks that (for a reasonable fee) will pretend they just received the cash in payment for oil and can absorb it that

way through their local commercial banks. But, frankly, if you're looking to launder large amounts of cash, thinking that private offshore banks in tax-haven jurisdictions as being the place to go speaks volumes on how much you really don't know about the "facts of life" in banking.

So why is there such an international ruckus in the press about money laundering in those "sleazy" offshore banks?

To understand this one must grasp the unseen fact and reality of what is known as "The Third House." Now, lest I be dismissed as a personally-exploitive conspiracy-theorist who relies on enhancing a sense of polarization between the "haves" and the "have-nots" and who refuses to grasp the ultimate realities of economic law (as a Canadian friend and former colleague of mine recently suggested in a publicly-circulated private memorandum to First Bank's Board of Directors, albeit not copied to me), let me first say that I am not without a modest amount of first-hand experience and perspective in matters of "The Third House."

Like many bright boys who grew up in "Leave It To Beaver's" America, by the age of thirteen I knew exactly what I wanted to be when I grew up: I wanted to be President of the United States. And so it was that I humbly and graciously accepted the office of President of the Eighth Grade Graduating Class and had my mother help me write the necessary graduation speech.

Likewise, in high school, I also humbly and graciously accepted the offices of Boys Club President and Student Body President (although I no longer needed my mother's assistance in speech-writing, already being an experienced veteran in such matters).

Perhaps it is little wonder, then (given my ultimate career aspirations), that in high school I became a devoted student of American government and history. This interest carried with me into college, where I also humbly and graciously accepted the office of Student Senator, then as Comptroller of the student's association, then as Student Body President.

While serving as president, I met with my counter-parts throughout the state's nearly thirty other institutions of higher learning and helped institute an inter-collegiate student lobby before the state's legislature.

In the year following my term as Student Body President, I humbly and graciously accepted the position as Director of the inter-collegiate student lobby, recruited a team of able and articulate assistants from several different colleges and then made my way to set up offices in the state's capitol city, eager to prove myself in the realm of intellect, reason, principle and inspiration.

It was to be a short legislative session that year and Mike, my student lobby director predecessor, told me I should be sure to check in with Lou, the head of the AFL-CIO's lobby, who would give me some helpful pointers on how to get things done. I humbly and graciously thanked him for the suggestion and mentally filed it somewhere under the category of "Don't Go Wasting My Time—There's Enough to Do Already."

After getting our offices set up and business cards printed, my assistants and I eagerly tore into all proposed laws effecting higher education and wasted no time in writing brilliant position papers, then circulating them to every elected member of either the state's House of Representatives or Senate, depending upon where a particular bill had been referred to committee for consideration. We also analyzed the past voting records of each member of either of the two legislative houses, identified those elected legislators who seemed to have the most pro-student voting records and then divided up "personal lobbying" responsibilities as related to them.

Russ, one of my able assistants, came rushing back to the office positively gushing over his stunning success in meeting with one such state senator named Pete, a true friend to students who even wanted us to call him by his first name and who had taken a real shine to Russ and had volunteered to personally sponsor any piece of legislation we cared to submit. Even more, Pete would then have the senate's own special team of researchers and draftsmen prepare the bills we wanted to submit. All we had to do is sketch out the basic items of concern to us and an official bill would be drafted for submission to the floor of the House and/ or the Senate and then referred to the appropriate committees. And that wasn't the end of it—Pete would even arrange for some co-sponsors of the legislation from the other legislative house (the House of Representatives), since there wasn't much sitting time for the legislature this year.

Upon hearing this report I all but fell off my executive chair (which, fortunately, had arms on it so that I could hold on and not make a spectacle of myself). I was so overwhelmed and so proud of what we had been able to accomplish in so short a time that I didn't know whether to dance or just cry for the joy and thrill of it all. Not wanting to betray what I feared was my near-obvious lack of experience and professionalism in such matters, I offered Russ my congratulations and allowed time for the office jubilation to run its course for a few minutes before reassuming my guiding role in our little band of warriors for the cause of students. Finally, I managed a, "Well, looks like we have work to do" type of comment, whereupon my team of able, articulate student advocates dove back into the position papers we had written on so many pieces of pending legislation to cull out and to categorize the crucial points we felt needed to be specifically addressed in law.

By morning Russ held in his hands three sheets of paper that neatly summarized the agenda areas of the state's collegiate students in 1972. By noon Pete had those same three sheets of paper. Within two days two different pieces of legislation had been drafted based on those three sheets of paper, and within four days there were a dozen or more co-sponsors for each of those pieces of legislation—Pete had been a man of his word.

These bills were quickly introduced on the floors of both houses and referred to the appropriate committees for consideration. We were "on our way" to accomplishing meaningful things on behalf of students.

Days turned into one week, then two weeks, then three weeks. Our bills were not scheduled for hearing by the committees. And while the committee chairmen were polite enough to take our personal visits and seemed genuinely understanding of and sympathetic toward what we were wanting to have considered, things were going no where fast. Finally, a bill we had previously written a position paper concerning (not one of our bills) was scheduled for hearing. We showed up and I gave eloquent testimony before the committee.

When I left the committee hearing I was greeted with television cameras, microphones and reporters in search of some sound and video bites for the evening news as related to legislative developments. I politely kept my cigar in my pocket (in college I had taken up pipe smoking, in keeping with the style of my professors of history and political science; at the state's capitol I had taken to smoking cigars, in keeping with the style of those who seemed to be the political shakers and movers). I gave my interviews so that by evening I could enjoy my 45-seconds of television fame via the evening news. As I was walking away from the TV cameras I was tapped on the shoulder and turned around expecting to find a radio or newspaper journalist who might have had a follow-up question. Instead, I was greeted by a man with no microphone, no note pad—just a middle-aged man in a suit. He introduced himself as if I should recognize his name and pointed to his lapel pin of the Roman numeral three.

My mind was a total blank. And so he started over. And although it is nearly thirty years ago, I quite clearly remember that conversation with Lou, who was the then director of the state lobby of the AFL-CIO (America's largest labor union). He asked me if Mike (my predecessor) had neglected to tell me to check in with him. I admitted that Mike had mentioned it, but with the shortness of the legislative session and with all the work there was to be done, I simply hadn't found the time. He then complimented Mike, saying that he seemed like a good kid who knew how to "play ball" but who should have clued me in. Mike was anything but an athlete, so I assumed Lou's reference to "playing ball" was speaking of something else, although I still wasn't "getting it."

I think Lou recognized my blank stare. He pointed again to the lapel pin he was wearing and said, "The Third House, son. We have a motto. 'Nothing passes without the Third House's okay.' It's that way in this state and it's that way on the national level too."

I must have still looked like he was speaking in a foreign language, so he patiently told me that lobbyists make up the "Third House" of any legislature. He explained that in our state, the primary controllers of the Third House were the labor lobbies (of which AFL-CIO was the main), the insurance lobby and the banking lobby, although all other lobbyists were welcome to participate, from the state's dairy farmers to the bar association to the American Medical Association to the restaurant association to you name it, including the inter-collegiate student lobby.

Lou explained that he was the unofficial head of the Third House and had been for some time. He said that he'd been keeping up with my group's activities since we arrived in the state's capitol and had been wondering why we hadn't checked in to ask for real help. There was now only a couple weeks left in the legislative session and all of our hard work and energy would soon end in nothing, if I didn't catch on soon. One of the two bills Pete had co-sponsored for us was fine with him, although Lou didn't particularly like the other piece of legislation as he felt it would tend to compromise some of what the American Federation of Teachers was attempting to accomplish. He said if we really wanted to have that bill debated in committee so we could make a show of our position, he would arrange it, but it would be wasted energy. And as to the bill he didn't mind, he would see it brought to consideration by committee and passed, if we would come out from a student position in favor of another piece of legislation the Third House had determined to see passed.

I asked about this other piece of legislation; he briefly described it to me. I told Lou that it really had nothing to do with college student priorities and we were committed to a simple focus. He then complimented me on what a great position paper writer I was and suggested that I "find an angle" and climb on-board. He then explained his expectations in three short words: "Quid pro quo," kindly suggesting that if I wanted to get very far in politics and in life, I should maybe learn the meaning of the term.

I agreed to "find an angle" on the one piece of legislation if Lou would get the "acceptable" piece of student legislation passed. I no longer remember what either piece of legislation was about. I do remember that as I left that meeting with Lou, I reached into my pocket and tossed my cigar into a dumpster and went to purchase a package of cigarettes. And it was on Capitol Hill of that state's capitol city that I marked my twenty-first birthday—not with a party, but with a disillusioned "Happy Birthday" drink that my oldest brother came to buy me in an effort to cheer me up, as I had (along with the cigar) tossed my "Leave It To Beaver" idealistic political career aspirations into a dumpster of disgust and no longer had a clue about what to do with my life.

And what does the Third House have to do with my "Practical Guide to Money Laundering?"

Four letters: OECD—the Organization for Economic Cooperation and Development. In April 1998 its Executive Council published a report on "Harmful Tax Competition", a report that pointed out the evils of tax haven jurisdictions attempting to do for their own national good those things that the developed nations have long done internationally.

Am I suggesting that the Third House has lobbyists devoted to the OECD? No—although it wouldn't surprise me; I'll say that much. What I look at in this is simply what the OECD is—it is a collection of developed nations that seek to rule the world economically. The OECD's modus operandi is closely akin to the concept of quid pro quo, although not nearly so subtle; it has reduced itself not to veiled threats against those nations that dare to defy the OECD's will, but to the promise of direct economic sanctions against those pesky, rebellious developing countries that won't toe the line set by their former colonial masters.

That being said—who sets the real national policies of the leading democratically governed OECD nations? Presumably, the congresses, parliaments and executive governments of the respective nations control their national and international policies. And what is it that I learned so vividly in my college years about who is really in control of the various legislative agendas of such nations (what they don't teach high school and college youth)?

I was explaining to a friend of mine recently that the official position of regulatory government in the developed nations was against common people taking advantage of offshore banking, based on the concept of such individuals being irresponsible tax evaders, when the home governments wanted to collect the maximum amount of tax revenues on income that was being earned. My friend pointed out (as I had done two years previously in an open letter criticizing the OECD's "Harmful Tax Competition" report) that this made no sense at all, given that additional earnings would likely be repatriated to the home jurisdictions so as to afford such citizens an ability to take a more active role in the general economies of their countries—economic activities that would all be taxable to the benefit of those governments themselves.

I chuckled and accused my friend of trying to be logical about it. One of the basic ways one of the most powerful and well-funded lobbies in America (the American Bankers Association) can move the American government to do its bidding is to supply quote-filled, well-worded position statements on how harmful tax haven competition is to America (when previously it was able to enact a law for Internal Revenue Service (national income tax) enforcement that honored and respected all foreigner capital deposits in the United States with tax-exempt status). Simply put, America's bankers have a vested interest—that interest being the maximum flow of deposits into their banks and the minimum flow of deposits out of their banks. How they suggest the wording of a position paper at the moment (the "angle") is of little importance. What they have decided to achieve is worth any price that may be paid in terms of logic or integrity as concerning individual rights.

Over a hundred years ago the then head of the House of Rothschild said it quite succinctly: "Give me control over a nation's currency, and I care not who makes its laws." Why would he say such a thing? Doesn't it matter whom a country elects to its parliament or congress? Doesn't it matter who becomes president or prime minister? Perhaps in some social policy areas, it does matter (within limits allowed). But when it comes right down to it, control over a nation's currency and over its banking environment IS control over the economic life and will of its people (with or without taxation).

Want to destabilize an American presidency or the party in power? Raise the discount and prime interest rates so that the country is thrown into recession with seemingly runaway inflation with nothing the president or the congress can do to stop it. Then wait the couple years until the president is voted out of office and the people congratulate themselves on their fine choices for a new beginning- and encourage those beliefs by lowering the discount and prime interest rates and letting the economy revive itself.

And what does any of THIS have to do with money laundering? Nothing. It is just a view of the real power of economic control via orchestrated manipulations of the money supply and the banking environment.

How the term "money laundering" is loosely thrown about is but another element of such control. The move in the United States, for instance, has been to redefine the crime of money laundering to include income tax evasion (something that is not a criminal matter at all in many tax haven jurisdictions, while money laundering as we universally think of it is a criminal matter with them).

By this new blurred definition of "money laundering", has First Bank and/or Van Brink ever been involved with such? Well, since it is (or, at least, was) against the law in Grenada for any offshore bank to violate the banking privacy of its depositors by reporting anything concerning their interest earnings to the tax authorities in their home jurisdictions (and since such tax authorities don't send out copies of the tax return forms submitted by tax payers for verification by all offshore banks as to whether interest income may have been correctly reported by individual tax payers), it is literally impossible for any offshore banker to say he has never been involved with "money laundering" activities (under that expanded definition)—even if he has never taken one suitcase of money from some drug lord or organized crime family.

And what does this new blurry definition of money laundering have to do with the Third House? I don't know. Maybe nothing. But something Lou said to me on the event of my graduation into life has stuck with me: "Nothing passes without the Third House's okay." I didn't believe he was lying then.

And I'm certain that lobbyists continue to play incredible behind-the-scenes roles in the formations of governmental national and international policies.

As for me, I keep betting on intellect, reason, principle and inspiration.

Do I seek to exploit the polarized positions of the "have's" and the "have nots?" No. I believe enough polarization already exists and that we need to consciously move to put aside the politics of fear—politics where someone trying to bring and share abundance with others is painted to be a public enemy and criminal—and along with that also put aside the politics of blaming our personal or societal woes on grand conspiracies of any kind.

Does this mean that frauds, thieves and con artists do not exist? No. Does this mean that there are no grand conspiracies at work? No. It simply means we need to "wise up" and do all that we by way of intellect, reason, principle and inspiration can do—and that as we consciously make choices on this basis and encourage others to do the same, we can know that the ripple effects in consciousness do change the world.

◆   ◆   ◆

Postscript:

I was so happy when I finished writing this "Practical Guide to Money Laundering" that I couldn't wait to share it with a friend. My friend read it, then said it sounded a little bitter. Was I really so bitter?

I don't think of myself as bitter (but would there be a bitter person who does?—Hmmm.). I think of myself as someone who nearly has his "eyes wide open" in terms of certain ways of the existing paradigm and who wants with all his heart to help bring about a shift in that consciousness. Yet I also recognize in myself something of "The Old Man's Song", as I call it—popularized by Frank Sinatra and containing the lines, "…Yes there were times/I'm sure you knew/ when I bit off more than I could chew/and through it all, when there was doubt/ I ate it up and spit it out/the record shows I took the blows…" or something to that effect, with a little "and I stood tall" thrown in.

—Van A. Brink

About the Author

Educated in Paris and London, Owen Platt is the author of a number of books, including the story of the Duke of Windsor's exile in The Bahamas during World War II *The Royal Governor and The Duchess*, a history of the D-Day deception *Bodyguard for Overlord* and the story of drugs, money and politics in The Bahamas *Paradise Lost* as well as a book of children's stories *The Truant Mermaid*.

A regular contributor to a number of offshore financial publications, he has been a director of several investment companies and has served on the board of a (legitimate!) Caribbean bank.

He lives and works in France and in The Caribbean.

0-595-65755-9

CPSIA information can be obtained
at www.ICGtesting.com
Printed in the USA
BVHW031910270919
559284BV00007B/17/P

9 780595 657551